PASTORAL THEOLOGY
IN THE CLASSICAL TRADITION

Andrew Purves

Westminster John Knox Press
LOUISVILLE
LONDON • LEIDEN

Book design by Sharon Adams
Cover design by Eric Walljasper

First edition
Published by Westminster John Knox Press
Louisville, Kentucky

This book is printed on acid-free paper that meets the American National Standards Institute Z39.48 standard. ∞

PRINTED IN THE UNITED STATES OF AMERICA

01 02 03 04 05 06 07 08 09 10   10 9 8 7 6 5 4 3 2 1

Library of Congress Cataloging-in-Publication Data

Purves, Andrew, 1946–
    Pastoral theology in the classical tradition / Andrew Purves.— 1st ed.
        p. cm.
    Includes index.
    ISBN 0-664-22241-2 (alk. paper)
        1. Pastoral theology—History of doctrines. I. Title.

    BV4006 .P87 2001
    253'.09—dc21   2001026567

Dedicated to my friend and colleague Charles Partee,
with warm affection and deep respect

Contents

Introduction

The Case for a Classical
Tradition in Pastoral Theology

PASTORAL CARE AS A THEOLOGICAL DISCIPLINE

It was a dark, cold winter night when I was called to the home of a member of my former congregation. Many years earlier I had left the congregation of which she was a member to teach at the seminary. The pastor who followed me had himself recently moved to a new call. Without a pastor, the family asked if I would be willing to make a call on the woman who was thought to be near death. Entering the house I greeted the assembled members of the extended family, all members of the congregation I once served. The gathered hush among this large family indicated that the situation was serious. The oldest daughter led me into her mother's bedroom, said a few quiet words of transition, and quickly left us alone.

The elderly woman before me clearly was very weak, but she clutched my hand with intensity and drew me close. I sensed both her affection and trust and my own deep awareness of pastoral responsibility. With hoarse words between harshly drawn breaths, she wanted assurance of her salvation. She told me that she knew she was dying. Above all else, she said, she needed to hear again the great evangelical affirmations of grace, redemption, and hope; the words are mine, but her intent was unambiguous. Put a different way, my former parishioner wanted a reminder of the reality and truth behind the central doctrines of the Christian faith as they applied to her life at the point of her death. Empathy with her and psychological sensitivity were appropriate, but more was required. The situation demanded a clear affirmation and application of Christian faith. I assured her of her salvation, prayed with her, and, laying my hands on her head, blessed her, committing her into the arms of her Savior.

Competent pastors have always recognized the strongest connection between what Christian faith confesses about God—redemption in and through Jesus Christ, and the life of sanctification—on the one hand, and the care of God's people, on the other. Competent theologians have known, too, that the theology taught and confessed in classroom and sanctuary is rich material for a person-sensitive pastor to mold and shape so that it applies appropriately to the situations of life and death that pastoral work confronts daily. John Calvin used to insist, for example, that pastoral care (or church discipline, as he called it) was not something alongside Word and sacrament, not a third thing. Calvin understood that the content of the gospel given in and through Word and sacrament as the primary means of grace was the working material for Christian pastoral work. No doubt interpersonal skills need to be learned; likewise, the competent pastor knows about human feelings, human development, and the complexities of human relationships.

But none of these factors supplies the basic content that gives pastoral work its specific Christian identity. That grounding comes from the content of faith itself, for the grace of God in Christ for us exposes the depth of the human condition in its separation from God in a way that no human science can. This same grace offers a remedy that leads to healing, blessing, and salvation to eternal life in union with Christ. The strongest possible connection exists between pulpit and counseling room, and between the study of Christian theology and the practice of pastoral care. Competent pastors and theologians have always known about this bond, and have integrated it in such a way that the great pastors were theologians, and the great theologians were pastors. Thus, when students ask me for advice on becoming a faithful pastor, I always tell them to become, first, students of the great theologians of the faith, and to learn from them what being a faithful pastor requires. Being a pastor demands also being a theologian, one who speaks and lives out of the center of the ecumenical, evangelical faith of the church.

In modern times some kind of a rift has opened up between being a pastor and being a theologian, as if a person could be one without the other. While recognizing the danger of generalization, I detect today a lack of confidence among pastors in the efficacy of Word and sacraments to effect healing and blessing, as well as a failure among theologians to present the gospel in a manner that allows pastors to discern directly the pastoral power of the Word of God.[1] Pastoral work is concerned always with the gospel of God's redemption in and through Jesus Christ, no matter the problem that someone presents. Pastoral work by definition connects the gospel story—the truths and realities of God's saving economy—with the actual lives and situations of people. Biblical and theological perspectives guide all pastoral work, and these perspectives, properly rooted in the gospel of salvation, are discovered to be inherently pastoral.

Biblical and theological perspectives, however, no longer shape the practice of much pastoral work. The modern pastoral care movement within the North American Protestant theological academy by and large revolves around psychological categories regarding human experience and symbolic interpretations about God. A relatively comfortable synthesis results in which pastoral theology, and, consequently, pastoral practice in the church, have become concerned largely with questions of meaning rather than truth, acceptable functioning rather than discipleship, and a concern for self-actualization and self-realization rather than salvation.[2] In view of these developments, perhaps the most important and provocative conclusion to come from a thoughtful reading of the classical tradition in pastoral theology is the discovery of theological realism. The classical pastoral writers, as we shall see, really did believe that theological statements made truthful reference to God, and that these statements had primary consequences for the understanding of human life and its healing and well-being. The contrast between the classical pastoral writers and much pastoral work today entails at least the awareness then and the loss now of the transcendence, objectivity, and reality of God, especially of a christological and soteriological clarity, and the insistence today that talk of God be assigned to the realm of myth and meaning. The understanding of humanity standing before God today, on this account, is given only in term of expressions of collective experience or states of inner consciousness.[3] A reading of the classical pastoral writers gives us cause for critical thought concerning the purpose of pastoral work as practiced today, including our ways of claiming to know God and to live rightly before God. The classical pastoral writers, in other words, deconstruct our theological subjectivity and its concomitant pastoral anthropology by insisting on the capacity of Christian doctrine to really talk about God truthfully and the need to guide the souls of the people accordingly.

The study of ancient texts in pastoral theology is not an end in itself, except perhaps for the pure historian. For the practical theologian, the focus is theology that is concerned with action, and in this case, the action of pastoral care in the context of today's church and society. While various scholarly conclusions may emerge from the review of ancient texts themselves, the more urgent question for us is to find out what these conclusions may mean for contemporary pastoral work. The task is not to "do pastoral care" the way the classical writers did. That option is hardly realistic or legitimate. The task, rather, is to allow these classical texts to provoke us into critical thinking by disturbing our calm, culture-bound assumptions concerning ministry. Having used these texts with Master of Divinity and Doctor of Ministry students and with groups of clergy, I have discovered that the texts speak for themselves; they raise issues for pastoral work today, often in direct, disturbing, and dramatic ways. This volume does not include the texts themselves, but readers should seek out these texts. I would hope that the selections would disturb readers in helpful and provocative ways.

The classical writers perceived things differently—for all manner of reasons. Such ways of looking, as far as we are concerned, may be rather odd by present standards, yet their perspectives allow us a curious angle of vision. Our view of the tasks and practices of pastoral care are reframed. Old questions are asked once again. New questions we have perhaps assumed we were not allowed to ask may be put forward for the first time. Discoveries may be made. If nothing else, the review of old texts in pastoral theology may force us to pause, to ponder, and to reflect in a critical way about our actions today as pastors. In this way we follow the counsel of C. S. Lewis, who once noted that the books of the past can help us because they challenge our presuppositions by offering a point of view outside of our cultural and historical framework. For this reason, he adds, we should read one old book for every new book![4] Perceiving the care of persons before God in the light of Jesus Christ through a study of the great pastors of Christian tradition affords us an angle of insight that at least may force us to question perceptions and assumptions that shape our own pastoral work.

My conviction is that the basic reconstitutive task for pastoral theology today is to establish once again the fundamental connection between the Christian doctrines of God, redemption, and hope, and the pastoral ministry of the church. To my mind, reestablishing this connection is the single most important conclusion that can come from the study of classical texts in pastoral theology. Why does Gregory of Nazianzus insert a section on the doctrine of the Trinity in the middle of his treatise on pastoral care? Why did John Chrysostom go to great lengths to try to avoid ordination? Why is Gregory the Great so concerned with the spirituality of the pastor? Why does Martin Bucer labor over the doctrine of sin and redemption in his understanding of true pastoral care? Why is Richard Baxter a pastoral evangelist? The short answer is that these pastoral theologians understood that pastoral ministry is the lived action in and through the church by the power of the Holy Spirit of the ministering reality of God in Christ for salvation. For them, pastoral care is lived out doctrine at the points of connection between the Gospel and the lives of God's people.

This book is written in the context of what I perceive to be a general lack of awareness among pastors today of the ecumenical evangelical Christian pastoral practice that was concerned above all with people in their relationship with God. Unlike most twentieth-century pastoral practice, dominated by psychological theory and oriented towards self-realization, classical pastoral care was much more obviously constrained by matters of theology—indeed, by matters of doctrine. The classical pastoral writers believed deeply that the active reality of God in Christ through the Holy Spirit was a present help in time of trouble. Moreover, pastoral care always had in focus the principal concern for the salvation of the sinner. In the classical tradition, then, pastoral theology and the practice of pastoral care give primary attention to God in Jesus Christ as the source of life, meaning, and the church's ministries of care. A central task of pastoral theology, then, is to remind the church that Jesus Christ is the pastor, the one who is the primary pastoral actor—who guides us to streams of living water, who forgives us our sins and saves us, who heals all our hurts, and who brings life out of death. The ministry of the church is, by the Holy Spirit, a sharing in the ministry of Christ. Ministry can have no other basis. A study of the texts of the great pastors of the past puts this front and square.

PASTORAL THEOLOGY IN HISTORICAL PERSPECTIVE

Apart from a handful of efforts scattered over the last forty years, from J. T. McNeill, W. A. Clebsch and C. R. Jaekle, Thomas C. Oden, Brooks Holifield, and to a lesser extent Seward Hiltner, "the history of pastoral care is largely unclaimed and unknown" today.[5] Contemporary pastoral care is, by and large, uninformed by historical practice.[6] One consequence is that much pastoral work today is disaffiliated from the church's theological heritage. Some observers suggest, for example, that much of what passes for pastoral practice is theologically and practically incoherent.[7] I believe we have entered a period characterized by the need for a profound reappraisal of core working assumptions in pastoral theology.

Pastoral theology began as an incidental discipline. Theologians and pastors did not at first set out to improve the work of ministry by writing systematic handbooks of pastoral care. Rather, theological reflection on pastoral ministry appears to have developed in response to needs that emerged in the coming together of human concerns within the context of the development of Christianity amidst the wider social and political world setting of the early church. The Second Letter of Clement (ca. 150), for example, was written to sustain Christians as they faced the expected imminent end of the world. The Latin Christian Tertullian of Carthage (d. 220) wrote about the pastoral process of penance and the external act by which sin should be dealt with, a procedure he called *exomologesis*. Cyprian wrote a letter (ca. 250) exhorting people to die as martyrs rather than denounce their faith.[8] Pastoral theology was occasional and contextual, written as circumstances required. In fact, not until 590, with the publication of Gregory the Great's *Book of Pastoral Rule*, did something like a comprehensive pastoral care textbook become available for the church. Recent attempts to uncover the wisdom of the classical tradition in pastoral care, by Oden and Volz,[9] for example, have been helpful in making a rather scattered, extensive, and somewhat inaccessible body of work available to students and pastors.

Alongside this, another trajectory was developing. While molding the pastoral mind and shaping the pastoral practice of the church in a profound and enduring manner, however, this path is largely unknown or neglected today, at least in much of the recent writing on pastoral care in the English-speaking church.[10] The primary concern of this trajectory was not with appropriate Christian responses to pastoral needs as they arose, but with the nature and responsibility of the pastoral or priestly office itself. In this sense it was a more basic or foundational inquiry. The controlling questions were not pragmatic or functional, valid as these are, but theological and spiritual. Gregory (d. 389) of Nazianzus's treatise *In Defense of His Flight to Pontus, and His Return, After His Ordination to the Priesthood, With an Exposition of the Character of the Priestly Office* is the jewel in the crown of patristic pastoral theology in this regard. Gregory's work served as the basis for two subsequent works, John (d. 407) Chrysostom's treatise *Six Books on the Priesthood*,[11] and, over two hundred years later, Pope Gregory (d. 604) the Great's *Book of Pastoral Rule*. Marked features of this trajectory include (1) a high view of the calling to ministry and a consequential awareness of one's unfitness for office; and (2) a sense of the extraordinary complexity of and sacrifice demanded by the pastoral office and a subsequent awareness of the depth of intellectual, moral, and spiritual preparation that is required.

Protestants now recognize that the Reformation itself had deeply pastoral roots. The concern was not for the reformation of doctrine and the church as such, but for the care of people in their lives before God, with the realization that thinking wrongly about God leads us to live wrongly. The reformers understood that thinking about God is a profoundly practical and pastoral matter. In keeping with the understanding of the Fathers of the church, the reformers also understood that all dogmatic theology is inevitably pastoral theology. However, Martin Bucer, the reformer of Strasbourg, alone in this period wrote a systematic treatise on pastoral care, a work long denied to English-speaking students of ministry. The Protestant approach to pastoral work was brought to magnificent expression and practice one century later in the work of the seventeenth-century English Puritan, Richard Baxter.[12]

DOES A CLASSICAL TRADITION EXIST?

This book examines Christian writers from the past who together represent what I call here the classical tradition in pastoral theology—"classical" in the sense that these writers, and the texts associated with them, have together shaped in enduring ways the minds and practices of pastors. As the English theologian James I. Packer wrote in his study of the Puritans, "Learning from the heroes of the Christian past is in any case an important dimension of that edifying fellowship for which the proper name is the communion of saints."[13] Texts from the fourth and sixth centuries— by Gregory of Nazianzus, John Chrysostom, and Gregory the Great, respectively—are still in print, in some cases in new translations. The text of the reformer Martin Bucer may soon be available in English for the first time. Richard Baxter's *The Reformed Pastor* is a perennially well-sold and widely read Puritan classic.

The texts discussed move from two Greek Fathers of the fourth century, to a Latin Father at the close of the sixth, to a Reformer of the sixteenth, and end with a Puritan divine of the seventeenth. As I present this material at conferences for clergy, and to Doctor of Ministry students, I am asked continually why seminary students are not introduced to this material. Both the classical pastoral authors and their texts are largely unknown today. Each chapter to follow, therefore, introduces the classical pastoral author in a brief biography. I then give a summary of major themes in his theology in general. The largest part of each chapter presents the author's pastoral theology, interweaving throughout a discussion of issues arising for pastoral work today. The conclusion pulls the volume together to highlight the salient lessons that come from studying the classical tradition in pastoral theology. The book ends with an epilogue, an ordination sermon. This sermon illustrates the significance of the classical tradition in pastoral theology, in which the lessons learned from these pastors from the past may be applied to pastors today at the very beginning of their ministry.

The texts I have selected do not represent an ecumenical tradition that agrees on all points. In fact, much distinguishes them, for the authors of these texts speak historically from Orthodox, Roman, Reformation, and Puritan perspectives. But in their rootedness in scripture, their theological perspicuity, their soteriological insistence, their sense of spiritual preparedness for ministry, their understanding of the complexities and demands of the pastoral office, and their awareness of God at work through the pastor in the lives of God's people, they have much in common. As we will see, enough commonality is present to suggest a tradition, a broad consensus concerning the essential focus of pastoral work in any age.

No doubt some readers will question the exclusion of other texts. Why no presentation of Augustine on marriage, or Luther on doubt, or Bushnell on religious development, for example? And why are texts written by women absent? My answer may not satisfy everyone: I wanted to treat texts that were written on the general work of pastoral care, rather than on specific topics, in the belief that these texts have had a foundational impact on the ministry of the church. I have no doubt that another book should address the issues raised by these questions.

No one is an expert on such a large swath of church history, but each of these areas and each of these theologians has its own experts. These scholars will have their own expert opinions on the treatment of any one text, but not on them all. Thus I am making a plea for the legitimacy of a generalist who relies upon the experts, but who, because of the generalist cast of mind, is able to look for connections that no expert in his or her right mind would dare to seek. But, then, pastors are by the nature of their calling generalists; presumably, pastoral theologians, too, may be allowed that special grace to know a little about a lot, rather than a lot about less and less.

1

Gregory of Nazianzus
"In Defense of His Flight to Pontus"

The scope of our art is to provide the soul with wings, to rescue it
from the world and give it to God, and to watch over that which is
in His image, if it abides, to take it by the hand, if it is in danger,
or restore it, if ruined, to make Christ to dwell in the heart by the
Spirit: and, in short, to deify, and bestow heavenly bliss upon, one
who belongs to the heavenly host.

Gregory of Nazianzus, *Oration* 2.22*

A man must himself be cleansed, before cleansing others: himself
become wise, that he may make others wise; become light, and
then give light: draw near to God, and so bring others near; be hallowed, then hallow them; be possessed of hands to lead others by
the hand, of wisdom to give advice.

Gregory of Nazianzus, *Oration* 2.71

Rightly so, the three Cappadocian Fathers of the second half of the fourth
century—Basil of Caesarea; his brother, Gregory of Nyssa; and Basil's
friend, Gregory of Nazianzus—are known as defenders of Nicene orthodoxy. They belong to the generation that followed and was indebted to
Athanasius and the bishops who wrote the Nicene Creed. What is not as
well known is that from the pen of Gregory of Nazianzus, ca. 463, came
that century's most influential writing on the challenges of the pastoral
office and the spiritual and moral qualities required of pastors. At the start

---

* The Greek text is found in Migne, *Patrologia Graeca*, vol. 35: 408–512. Citations
will be taken from Philip Schaff and Henry Wace, eds., *Nicene and Post-Nicene Fathers*,
Second Series, vol. 7 (Edinburgh: T. & T. Clark and Grand Rapids: Eerdmans, 1989).
References are to Oration 2, followed by paragraph number in *NPNF*, 2.7.

of his ministry Gregory outlined his understanding of the nature of priest-hood and the person of the priest in a text that helped shape the practice of the pastoral art in the succeeding generation through its impact on John Chrysostom. Nearly 230 years later Gregory's writing formed the basis for the pastoral theology of Pope Gregory the Great, whose work would then become the primary pastoral care text in the church until, one can argue, Martin Bucer's *Concerning the True Pastoral Care*, written in 1538.

GREGORY OF NAZIANZUS: A BRIEF BIOGRAPHY[1]

J. Quasten opens his account of Gregory with a sympathetic character assessment.

> He does not share the vigor of (Basil) nor his ability as a leader. . . . He preferred quiet contemplation and the union of ascetic piety and lit-erary culture to the splendor of an active life and ecclesiastical posi-tion. . . . He longs for solitude and yet the prayers of his friends, his accommodating disposition and his sense of duty call him back to the turbulent world and the controversies and conflicts of his time. Thus his entire career is a succession of flights from, and returns from, the world.[2]

Gregory's psychological makeup has been characterized in terms of the largely unresolved tension between the throne and the mountain, that is, between the demands of ecclesiastical responsibility and the longing for contemplative retreat.[3] Certainly his adult life was a journey between the search for truth (*theoria*) and the concern to meet the pastoral demands of ecclesiastical office (*praxis*). However we understand the tensions within Gregory himself, he clearly insisted that the practice of pastoral ministry be built on a spiritual, theological, and moral foundation. As he wrote in the *Oration*,

> how could I . . . clothe myself with the garb and name of priest, before my hands had been consecrated by holy works; before my eyes had been accustomed to gaze safely upon created things, with wonder only for the Creator, and without injury to the creature; before my ear had been sufficiently opened to the instruction of the Lord? (2.95)

Gregory was called "the Great" by the Ecumenical Council of Ephe-sus. He was also known as "the Theologian," according to the Council of Chalcedon, a title he shares in Eastern tradition only with the Apostle John. He was born around 330 at Arianzum, a country estate belonging to his father, in the neighborhood of Nazianzus in what today is central

Turkey. He did not lack in privilege.[4] His father was a bishop. His mother, Noona, had a decisive influence on the early training of her son: "I had been invited from my youth . . . and had been cast upon (God) from the womb, and presented by the promise of my mother" (2.77). Gregory evidently saw himself as one set apart for God, and from the world, considering himself an alien here on earth. As a child he had a vision in which two virgins named Chastity and Temperance appeared to him, inviting him to join them in the contemplation of the Trinity.[5] He felt henceforth called to a life of celibacy and asceticism. Later, as a youth on a sea journey to Athens, amid a serious storm—fearful of death and not yet baptized—he called out to God, promising himself entirely to God. His mother, he believed, had a vision of his danger, and by prayer stilled the storm.[6] Very early convictional experiences shaped the life to follow.

He received a thorough education in philosophy and rhetoric at home, in Caesarea, Alexandria, and finally in Athens. For all his life he retained a deep love of learning. In Athens he developed a life-long relationship with Basil (of Caesarea, "the Great"), whom he had met first in Alexandria. Although later their friendship was put to trial, as young men they were united in trust and friendship, encouraging one another in Christian discipline and learning. They made plans, in fact, to set up their own monastery after leaving Athens. Gregory was attracted to a monastic life of silence, and amid his later ecclesiastical duties he dreamed always of retiring to the desert or a mountain to fulfill his search for a deeper relationship with God. Elijah and John the Baptist inspired him. When Gregory left Athens around 357, however, he returned home, and was received into the church by baptism. While home, he lived an ascetic life combined with study and service. A year later Basil summoned him to share his monastic retreat in a wild desert place called Pontus.

> Nothing seemed to me so desirable as to close the doors of my senses, and, escaping from the flesh and the world . . . constantly growing more and more to be, a real unspotted mirror of God and divine things. . . . If any of you has been possessed by this longing, he knows what I mean and will sympathise with my feelings at that time. (2.7)

Gregory later recalled with joy the time that he spent with Basil.[7]

His father, however, needed his son at home to assist him with his episcopal duties. Aged and without the education of his son (Gregory praised his father more for his piety than for his theological ability[8]), Gregory the Elder had need of a coadjutor. Against his will, yet with the approval of the people of the diocese, Gregory was ordained to the priesthood by his father, probably on Christmas Day 361 or 362. He always felt his ordination was coercive—"an arbitrary act of oppression" (2.6), he called it. "I was so grieved by this act of tyranny," he wrote, "that I forgot everything: friends, parents, my native land and people. Like an ox stung by a gadfly, I returned to Pontus hoping to find a cure."[9] He fled from home to Basil's desert retreat near Epiphany.

Gregory, however, soon came to a new understanding of his duties, and by Easter had returned to his father. His explanation and defense of his flight occasioned the text that is the subject of our inquiry. Apparently the congregation was less than enthralled: "How slow you are, my friends and brethren, to listen to my words, though you are so swift in tyrannizing over me, and tearing me from my Citadel Solitude" (3.1). Probably never given *viva voce*, the *Defense* still remains a singularly important treatise on the pastoral office for its insights into the heart and soul of the person who would be a pastor, and of the difficulties of the office.

Around 371, nine or ten years later, the story virtually repeated itself when Gregory was consecrated by Basil, who was now metropolitan of Cappadocia, to the see of Sasima. Gregory called Sasima "a tiresome and cramped little village," a "stopping-place." Once again he was ordained against his will; once again he fled from the responsibilities of his ordination. "Again I weep and lament," he wrote.[10] On his return he remarked that "(I was hoping) to be free of practical affairs and to devote myself peacefully to the contemplative life."[11] His friendship with Basil never recovered its previous joy. Gregory visited Sasima but never entered the cathedral church, preferring to continue his work at home with his father. On the latter's death in 374, Gregory took over the administration of the diocese, until he withdrew a year later, as he put it, "like a fugitive,"[12] again to a contemplative vocation. Gregory clearly still had problems with the demands of public ecclesiastical life as the tension between the throne and the mountain remained unresolved. While he accepted the necessity of attending to pastoral duties, he found them unhelpful for his contemplative endeavors.[13] While on this retreat after his father's death, he heard the news of Basil's death, and he preached at his friend's funeral.

In 379 the small Nicene or "orthodox" minority at Constantinople invited him to be their bishop. Ironically, Constantinople was everything Gregory by nature rejected: worldliness, busyness, and political intrigue. Arian emperors and archbishops had oppressed and virtually crushed the see out of existence. He initially resisted the call, as we might expect, but accepted eventually, "not by my own will, but by the coercion of others."[14] This ministry, however, appears to have become an integrating experience for Gregory, and he threw himself into his duties with energy and creativity. The congregation met in a renovated house given the name "Anastasia" (Resurrection). For two years he was a notable and controversial figure around town, a champion of orthodoxy, his priority being the worship of the Trinity. During this time, in the summer or autumn of 380, he preached his famous *Five Orations on the Divinity of the Logos*, for which he received the title "the Theologian," "The Defender of the Godhead of the Word." Yet this was a violent time. Theology and politics were forged into competing camps as Arians and Orthodox fought for control of both the church and the empire. Not surprisingly, Gregory was under threat of assassination from his political and theological opponents.

With the accession in 381 of a new emperor, Theododius, Gregory was recognized formally as bishop of Constantinople and was led in triumph to the cathedral Church of the Apostles. At the Council of Constantinople, the hierarchy of Egypt and Macedonia—who opposed Gregory on his teaching on the divinity of the Holy Spirit—objected to his election on the ruse of questioning the canonicity of his transfer from the hated Sasima. Canon 15 of the Council of Nicaea forbade the migration of bishops from one see to another. Sickly, Gregory resigned his "throne" in disgust and returned to the "mountain," his home diocese in Nazianzus, until 384, when he retired to monastic life. "Give me my desert, my rural life, and my God," he said in his farewell address to the cathedral congregation.[15] He devoted the remaining years of his life to writing poetry and occasional theological treatises. He died somewhere between 389 and 391.

THEMES IN GREGORY'S THEOLOGY

In order to place Gregory's pastoral theology in a wider frame of reference, we will note (1) his view of the special calling to be a theologian/pastor; (2) the importance of "theosis," or "divinization" in his thinking; (3) his development of the doctrine of the Trinity in terms of relation of origin; (4) his insistence on the full humanity and divinity of Christ; and (5) his view of human nature.

A Special Call

"Not to every one, my friends, does it belong to philosophize about God" (27.3).[16] Gregory was aware that the theologian had to embody a quality of life and faith that was appropriate to the nature of God. "We will utter the divine Mysteries under our breath, and holy things in a holy manner. . . . Let even our disputings then be kept within bounds" (27.5). The theological self, he knew, must be polished to beauty (27.6). For Gregory, as for Athanasius before him, one can only come to know God in a godly way, for knowledge of God is possible only in a manner appropriate to the nature of God.[17] Keeping with Gregory's contemplative disposition, he notes that "it is necessary to be truly at leisure to know God."[18] Certainly one cannot do theology in a hurried, harried way; theology is a reflective discipline that takes time and is unlikely to flourish amid busyness. Pastors, Gregory insists, must have profound theological competence if they are to lead others faithfully (2.35–50) by contending on behalf of God (2.40). A significant part of that competence is the capacity to be "unbusy." A pastor needs a willingness to take the time to know God if he or she is to minister the things of God.

While Gregory by nature had the frame of mind and spirit that enabled him to be a theologian, a running theme throughout the "Flight to Pontus" is a deep sense of his own lack of personal qualifications for the work to which he was called. Gregory, for all of his theological brilliance and astonishing pastoral insights, remained a humble man, aware of his own need for the grace of God in order to accomplish the work of the gospel.

Deification

According to Gregory, the final goal of the Christian life that pastors must have in view for their people—the purpose for which they were created, from which they have fallen away, and for which they have been re-created by Christ—is a direct and dynamic relationship with God in the life to come. He calls this goal "deification," and he notes that the scope of the pastoral art is "to deify, and bestow heavenly bliss upon, one who belongs to the heavenly host" (2.22). Gregory does not understand deification, or *theosis*, in a speculative way. Rather, knowledge of God and of our future in and with God have as their object the God who has created the world and come among us in Jesus Christ in such a way that God is known as Creator and Redeemer. As Gregory outlines in his famous Oration on Holy Baptism (Or. 40), the acts of salvation history—creation and providence, incarnation, crucifixion, resurrection and ascension, the second coming and the final judgment—are for the overcoming of our separation from God and our restoration to unity with God (40.45). Thus, Gregory's theology is controlled by the divine economy to the end of anticipating a future life with God that will be permanent and filled with joy.[19]

Gregory developed the theological idea of "theosis" or "divinization" more aggressively than anyone before him, investing the concept with a dynamic soteriological, christological, and pastoral significance. This theme invests his pastoral theology through and through with soteriological and eschatological focus.

The Doctrine of the Trinity

While crediting Basil as his "teacher of dogma," Gregory surpassed his friend in at least two ways. First, in the *Theological Orations*, preached in Constantinople in 380, Gregory gives a particularly compelling account of the dynamic, relational nature of Nicene trinitarian theology as it was developing up to its consolidation at the Council of Constantinople in 381, and in so doing developed a theology of the Trinity in terms of relation of origin. Second, Gregory went beyond Basil, who had himself written a most significant book on the Holy Spirit, insofar as he was the first theologian to speak of the *homoousion* of the Holy Spirit.

Gregory was the first theologian to give a clear account of the distinctive characters of the divine persons as unoriginate, begotten, and procession (*agennesia, genesis, ekporeusis*). In so doing, he developed a theological—that is, a trinitarian—basis for personhood. The persons of the Trinity have their properties as properties of relation (*skesis*) of origin. The Father is a name of relation: "Father is not a name either of an essence or of an action. . . . It is the name of the Relation in which the Father stands to the Son, and the Son to the Father" (29.16). This conception was a departure from Nicene orthodoxy insofar as it posited relation with rather than procession from the being (*ousia*) of the Father. Gregory argued similarly regarding the Holy Spirit. Although the Son and the Spirit receive their deity from the Father, because the Father is source (*pege*) or cause (*arche*), Son and Spirit are not inferior.

Gregory also pushed beyond Basil to give clear expression to the *homoousion* of the Spirit. "Is the Spirit God? Most certainly. Well, then, is He Consubstantial? Yes, if He is God" (31.10). Thus the Father is Father precisely in his relation to the Son and the Spirit, and the Spirit and the Son are what they are precisely in their relations to the Father and to one another.[20] With this approach Gregory developed a dynamic, personal, and perichoretic construal in his understanding of the Trinity in terms of internal relations. Not being as such, but relations as communion form the ultimate ontological category by which we may apprehend the Christian doctrine of God as Holy Trinity, as three persons, one God, in which God is "divided without division," and "united in division" (39.11). For this reason, as one contemporary Orthodox theologian has written, "the person both as a concept and as a living reality is purely the product of patristic thought."[21] The implication is that the loss of the doctrine of the

Trinity means the loss of the basis for personhood. This insight is important for theological anthropology and pastoral theology.

Christology

Gregory was also the first of the Greek Fathers to apply trinitarian terminology to the christological formula, which led, by the following century, to the one person, two natures formula of Chalcedon.[22] In his first letter to Cledonius, Gregory notes that

> the Saviour is made of elements which are distinct from one another . . . yet He is not two Persons. God forbid! For both natures are one by the combination, the Deity being made Man, and the Manhood deified. . . . And I say different Elements, because it is the reverse of what is the case in the Trinity; for There we acknowledge different Persons so as not to confound the persons; but not different Elements, for the Three are One and the same in Godhead.[23]

Thus Gregory defended the complete humanity of Christ, including, against Apollinarianism, his having a human mind and soul. Gregory understood that a savior without a human mind and soul, and one who has not borne in his body the sin of the world, is no savior at all.

Anthropology

Gregory understood human beings as having a composite or double nature made up of flesh and spirit, or body and soul. When God made humankind, he wrote, God "mingled dust with spirit, and compounded an animal visible and invisible, temporal and immortal, earthly and heavenly, able to attain to God but not to comprehend Him, drawing near and yet afar off" (2.75).[24] This understanding of the human in his or her whole personhood is important to emphasize over and against dualistic anthropologies in which the human being is partitioned. While Gregory believes we have a 'higher' or spiritual nature and a 'lower' or fleshly nature, and while he indicates also that the image of God is found in the soul or mind, the whole person is the subject of God's salvation and the subject, therefore, of pastoral work. Gregory does not suggest that sin is the result of flesh. Interestingly, with regard to sin, Gregory maintains that the soul was disobedient, in spite of its divine origin, partaking of the heavenly nobility (2.17), and the flesh only cooperated and shared in its condemnation (2.23). Thus, salvation is not a matter for the soul only, but the body is the fellow heir of the soul, for the soul draws the body heavenward in an act in which the soul is to the body what God is to the soul.

THE PASTORAL THEOLOGY
OF GREGORY OF NAZIANZUS

In the *Second Oration*, "In Defense of His Flight," Gregory attempts to explain to his home congregation at Nazianzus why he fled from the responsibilities of the sacerdotal office immediately following his ordination. His defense is, more or less, a treatise on the priesthood and pastoral care that is readable at one extended sitting. No given divisions appear within the 117 paragraphs; rather, he weaves a seamless tapestry as he moves through his defense. (An outline is provided in the appendix to this chapter.) The *Oration* is a spiritually tuned and theologically considered defense of his behavior after his forced ordination. Certain issues arise in this text that have significance for pastoral work today: (1) the pastor as "physician of souls," which is Gregory's dominant metaphor for pastoral work; (2) the difficulties to be found in pastoral work; (3) the spiritual requirements for being a pastor; and (4) the issue of call and obedience, and the place of spiritual autobiography in preparation for ministry.[25]

The Pastor as a "Physician of Souls"

In the context of the now rather famous idea of pastoral care as "the art of arts" (2.16), Gregory draws a parallel between the physicians of souls (*iatroi psychoi*) and those who treat the ailments of the body, giving readers a metaphor for pastoral work. According to Gregory, the pastor is a healer, even more so than the physician, for the pastor treats a sickness that is a deeply subtle foe of healing, a sickness of soul. The pastor thus has the more difficult task, concerned as it is with

> the diagnosis and cure of our habits, passions, lives, wills, and whatever else is within us, by banishing from our compound nature (body and soul) everything brutal and fierce, and introducing and establishing in their stead what is gentle and dear to God. (2.18)

The goal of pastoral work, he notes, is the salvation and sanctification of a person, "to provide the soul with wings, to rescue it from the world and give it to God . . . in short, to deify, and bestow heavenly bliss upon, one who belongs to the heavenly host" (2.22). The pastor, guided by Christ, "a Shepherd to shepherds and a Guide to guides," is to so guide the flock that Christ himself presents the flock, spotless and worthy of heaven (2.117). Such a goal alone is deserving of a pastoral care that is worthy of the true Shepherd (2.34).

Drawing upon a soteriological theme from his theological anthropology, Gregory argued that the pastor's task is similar to that of the soul's relationship to the body: as the soul perfects the body, the pastor perfects the church (2.3). To our modern way of thinking, this rather odd notion reflects his philosophical milieu. Nevertheless, even if we cannot embrace the metaphysical imagery we can see that Gregory has identified a perennial pastoral issue. God, he suggests, has bound the body and soul together in order that a person may inherit the glory above by way of a struggle—wrestling with things below, tried as gold in a fire by things earthly—that through this struggle the soul may draw the body to itself and raise it to heaven. In this way, the soul is to the body what God is to the soul (2.17). The pastor, as the soul of the congregation, is given the extraordinary task of sharing in the work of deifying or making godly the people of God through a work of wrestling with sin and freeing a person from its grasp.

The pastor as a physician of souls must discern the wiles of the lower nature, acting at times against what amounts to "an armed resistance" on the part of those whom the pastor would help (2.19).

> For we either hide away our sin, cloaking it over in the depth of our soul, like some festering and malignant disease, as if by escaping the notice of men we could escape the mighty eye of God and justice. Or else we allege excuses in our sins, by devising pleas in defense of our falls, or tightly closing our ears, like the deaf adder that stoppeth her ears, we are obstinate in refusing to hear the voice of the charmer, and be treated with the medicines of wisdom, by which spiritual sickness if healed. Or, lastly, those of us who are most daring and self-willed shamelessly brazen out our sin before those who would heal it, marching with bared head, as the saying is, into all kinds of transgression. (2.20)

The battle, then, is with the

> hidden man of the heart, and our warfare is directed against that adversary and foe within us, who uses ourselves as his weapons against ourselves, and, most fearful of all, hands us over to the death of sin. (2.21)

This pastoral wrestling with sin in the parishioners' hearts is undertaken to the good end of liberation and freedom—what Gregory calls the bestowal of heavenly bliss upon one who belongs to the heavenly host (2.22). All of the law and the prophets testify to the need for this pastoral wrestling for this saving goal, Gregory suggests. This same goal is given in the incarnation of Jesus Christ and the gospel of our redemption in and through him. The whole gospel, then, is "a training from God for us, and a healing for our weakness, restoring the old Adam to the place whence he fell, and conducting us to the tree of life" (2.25). "Of this healing we, who are set over others, are ministers and fellow-labourers" (2.26). Further—and for Gregory, terrifyingly so—the burden of the salvation of a soul is upon the pastor: "[W]hat a struggle ought ours to be, and how great skill do we require to treat, or get men treated properly, and to change their life, and give up the clay to the spirit" (2.28).

Gregory's images of the relationships between the soul and the body, and the pastor and the congregation, are drawn from neo-Platonism and to modern eyes may read like an anthropology and a theory of ministry drawn from a previous age. We do not today see theological anthropology in such dualistic or hierarchical terms. Nor do Protestants see a pastor in his or her distinction to the congregation in such a manner, although the continuing use of the shepherding and pastoring metaphors carry over into ministry something of the profound yet unhelpful difference in kind between shepherd and sheep. Nevertheless, within the philosophical framework of his time, Gregory posits enduring truths for pastoral care: a pastor's care of people at once mirrors God's care for them, and carries precisely that authority; and the goal of pastoral care is nothing other than the salvation of the person to eternal bliss. Such a perspective puts all pastoral care into a godly, soteriological, and eschatological framework. This framework, we shall see, is characteristic of pastoral theology in the classical tradition.

Why does Gregory cast pastoral care into such a framework? The physician of souls, as we have noted, has to treat a sickness that lies deeply in "the hidden man of the heart" (2.21). This reference is not to superficial pains and human concerns, important as these aspects of life are. The concern is soteriological, lying now in people's profound and deadly separation from God. Gregory sees the human situation or condition in the light of what God had to do in order that we might be restored to health, or, in Gregory's language, to union with God. For our healing, then, were we given the gospel. The scope of the pastoral art, the goal of the physician of souls, is to contend on behalf of God and thereby to lead people back to God.

For Gregory, the magnitude of the pastoral office is no less than that God will hold pastors accountable for their pastoral care. Citing Ezekiel 3:18, Gregory states that God will require the people's souls at the pastor's hands (2.113). Small wonder he was terrified at the responsibility and initially fled from it: upon the pastor's efforts, he believed, the salvation of a soul is staked. Whether "destined for undying chastisement or praise, for its vice or virtue,—what a struggle ought ours to be" (2.28).

What is a pastor? Textbooks today lean heavily towards a functional or skills perspective. The result is an enormous gain in practical knowledge for competent pastoral care. Pastoral work today is largely, and usually appropriately, a work of brief counsel, comfort, and companionship, sometimes within a liturgical framework—baptism, weddings, funerals, Eucharists for homebound persons, and so on. These tasks are accomplished amid the busy round of administration of the congregation, its programs, and mission, not the least of which is attention to preaching and liturgical responsibilities.

What is missing today, however, is a central metaphor that holds the various pastoral tasks together by providing a sense of direction for or giving focus to pastoral work that has soteriological and eschatological significance. Failing to invest ministry with this significance fragments ministry and can trivialize pastoral work.

For Gregory of Nazianzus, the pastor is a physician of souls and is called by God to bring people to a godly healing of their sin and to a life of righteousness and virtue, to the end that they—pastor and people together—may say, "Glory, in Christ Jesus our Lord" (2.117). The usefulness of this metaphor is its indication that pastoral work has to do primarily with people in their relationship with God, and that every function of a pastor must be held accountable to the salvation that is given in Jesus Christ. While the soteriological and eschatological intentions behind the metaphor define pastoral work as having at its center the healing of soul, the metaphor itself is not especially helpful today. The word "physician" has been so claimed and defined by the medical field that I doubt it can be extended into pastoral work without a host of unhelpful and inappropriate assumptions. Neither is the word "soul" terribly useful today, harboring as it does an immaterial and unworldly connotation that is out of step with an embodied and community-based biblical anthropology. For Gregory, pastoral work remains *cura animarum*, the care of souls, and the pastor is a "physician of souls." While Gregory's intention in using this metaphor is a valuable corrective to much contemporary pastoral work that is devoid of soteriological and eschatological concerns, pastoral theology today urgently needs to find alternative metaphors that carry this same intention.

The Difficulties of Pastoral Work

We have already noted that the pastor must battle what Gregory called an "armed resistance" against the diagnosis and healing of sin. Gregory goes to considerable length to testify, correspondingly, to the complexities of pastoral work. According to Gregory, three factors complicate the pastoral task. First, people are different.

> For men and women, young and old, rich and poor, the sanguine and despondent, the sick and whole, rulers and ruled, the wise and ignorant, the cowardly and courageous, the wrathful and meek, the successful and failing, do not require the same instruction and encouragement. (2.28)

Further,

> some are led by doctrine, others trained by example; some need the spur, others the curb; some are sluggish and hard to rouse to the good, and must be stirred up by being smitten with the word; others are immoderately fervent in spirit, with impulses difficult to restrain, like thoroughbred colts, who run wide of the turning post, and to improve them the word must have a restraining and checking influence. (2.30)

Especially in matters of faith, says Gregory, the piety of the congregation itself causes problems for the pastor. People who believe something fervently but wrongheadedly are unlikely to take instruction graciously. If they are arrogant or ignorant or so open-minded that they are open to everything, the task of instruction is equally difficult. Teaching someone who is still fresh is far easier than trying to inscribe true doctrine on top of false inscriptions (2.43). In whatever case, the teacher of faith must

> apply to each a treatment suitable for it. . . . And since the common body of the church is composed of many different characters and minds, like a single animal compounded of discordant parts, it is absolutely necessary that its ruler should be at once simple in his uprightness in all respects, and as far as possible manifold and varied in his treatment of individuals, and in dealing with all in an appropriate and suitable manner. (2.44)

Some, then, must be fed with milk (simple doctrine), others with solid food (wisdom).

With these insights Gregory of Nazianzus anticipated by over two hundred years the more detailed and systematic contextual pastoral exposition of Gregory the Great. The point is that pastoral care must be person-specific, addressing the good news of the gospel to the nature, needs, and condition of the person for whom the pastor gives care.

A second complicating factor in the exercise of this complex ministry is the need for a pastor to be mindful of his or her own responsibilities. The pastor must keep careful balance in order to guide people in a manner appropriate to their needs and nature. Gregory takes it to be self-evident

> that just as it is not safe for those who walk on a lofty tightrope to lean to either side, for even though the inclination seems slight, it has no slight consequences, but their safety depends upon their perfect

> balance: so in the case of one of us, if he leans to either side, whether
> from vice or ignorance, no slight danger of a fall into sin is incurred,
> both for himself and those who are led by him. (2.35)

The obligations of spiritual, theological, and moral propriety are therefore enjoined.

> We must really walk in the King's highway, and take care not to turn
> aside from it either to the right hand or to the left. . . . For such is the
> case with our passions, and such in this matter is the task of the good
> shepherd, if he is to know properly the souls of his flock, and to guide
> them according to the methods of a pastoral care which is right and
> just, and worthy of the true Shepherd. (2.35)

(The spiritual preparation required of the pastor is the focus of the next
section of this essay.)

A third factor that complicates pastoral work arises in the context of the
pastor's primary task of "the distribution of the word" (2.35). Gregory
reflects at length on the relationship between doctrine and pastoral care
and the complexities that arise for pastoral work. First, not everyone is
able to interpret scripture in a pastorally appropriate manner. "To me
indeed it seems no slight task, and one requiring no little spiritual power,
to give in due season to each his portion of the word, and to regulate with
judgment the truth of our opinions" (2.35). Further, because pastors are
involved with matters of such eternal importance, theological competence
is a matter of evident necessity. In fact, Gregory believes that risks abound
for the pastor who does not teach the doctrine of God faithfully. Yet this,
too, demands no little ability, "especially before a large audience, com-
posed of every age and condition, and needing like an instrument of many
strings, to be played upon in various ways; or to find any form of words
able to edify them all, and illuminate them with the light of knowledge"
(2.39). Failure in understanding, speech, or hearing leads to a maiming of
the truth.

The godly pastor is not only a psychologist and a rhetorician, but above
all else also must be a theologian. Gregory shows this in several ways. First,
evidence of Gregory's own familiarity with the Bible is found in every
paragraph of his treatise; biblical allusions and references, as well as frequent citations, are seamlessly written into the text. The classical tradition
in pastoral theology is characterized by such plain use of the biblical text
to illumine the responsibilities and challenges of the pastoral office. Second, Gregory upholds the virtue of orthodox doctrine: the pastor, having
undertaken to contend on behalf of God, must not lead people astray
because of theological ignorance. The pastor must be able to regulate pas-

toral opinions and guidance with the truth in regard to God (2.39). The pastor's duty is not to mix godly doctrine "with what is common and cheap, and debased, and stale, and tasteless, in order to turn the adulteration to our profit, and accommodate ourselves to those who meet us, and curry favor with everyone, becoming ventriloquists and chatterers" (2.46).

Gregory of Nazianzus does not separate theological and pastoral work. He is aware of a distinction between them, of course, for one is the study of God, and especially of the Trinity, while the other is the service of God through the pastor's care for God's people; nevertheless, the first implies or calls for the second, and the second is possible only on the basis of the first. One cannot be a pastor without being a theologian, in the sense of being a faithful and disciplined student of the Word of God. Gregory's view prevailed for a long time in the church, and probably only in recent times has pastoral work come to have such an ambiguous connection to the church's theological heritage that psychology and counseling methods rather than the church's doctrine have come to dominate.

In view of the competencies required for pastoral work, Gregory asks rhetorically, "Who is sufficient for these things?" (2.46), and "Who is the man?" (2.96, 97, and 98). Clearly, he reflects, the demands of the pastoral office are extraordinarily complex, leading even the most skilled individual surely to wonder whether he or she is competent. Pastoral work involves a blending of theological and spiritual knowledge, on the one hand, with psychological, rhetorical, and pedagogical skills, on the other. The competent and faithful pastor must know both God and people in such a way that he or she can interpret the significance of the gospel to meet every life situation and every manner of person, all to the glory of God and the eternal salvation of each person. These subtle attainments are not merely clinical or technical skills, the exercise of which is "the art of arts." A reading of Gregory's text is a timely reminder—both in his day and ours—that ministry should be entered into by those who recognize the need to commit themselves to the work of theology and who have the skill and sensitivity to understand the nature and needs of persons in such a way that the gospel can be addressed for them in healing and helpful ways.

Spiritual Requirements for Being a Pastor

According to Gregory, God has ordained that some people "should be pastors and teachers, for the perfecting of the church, those, I mean, who surpass the majority in virtue and nearness to God" (2.3). To this task Gregory did not feel himself qualified (2.9). Who would? Aware that one cannot undertake to heal others while being himself full of sores (2.13 and

2.70), the pastor is to "know no limits in goodness or spiritual progress, and should dwell upon the loss of what is still beyond him" (2.14). Again: pastors "should be of such virtue, so simple and modest, and in a word, so heavenly, that the gospel should make its way, no less by their character than by their preaching" (2.69). A pastor must "be cleansed, before cleansing others: himself become wise, that he may make others wise; become light, and then give light: draw near to God, and so allow others near; be hallowed, then hallow them; be possessed of hands to lead others by the hand, of wisdom to give advice" (2.71). "With these thoughts," he muses, "I am occupied night and day: they waste my marrow, and feed upon my flesh, and will not allow me to be confident or to look up" (2.71).

Gregory was deeply aware of the need for a profound commitment to moral and spiritual formation. Making reference to pastors who fail to be adequately prepared (throughout he has harsh words to say to pastors), and including himself in the observation, he notes how pastors "ordain ourselves men of heaven and seek to be called Rabbi by men; the letter is nowhere, everything is to be understood spiritually, and our dreams are utter drivel, and we should be annoyed if we were not lauded to excess." With heavy irony, he concludes that "this is the case with the better and more simple of us; what of those who are more spiritual and noble?" (2.49). In view of the spiritual, moral, and theological preparation required for ministry, and of the dangers when that preparation is inadequate,

> not even extreme old age would be too long a limit to assign. For hoary hairs combined with prudence are better than inexperienced youth, well reasoned hesitation than inconsiderate haste, and a brief reign than a long tyranny. . . . Who can mould, as clay figures are molded in a single day, the defender of the truth, who is to take his stand with Angels, and give glory with Archangels, and cause the sacrifice to ascend to the altar on high, and share the priesthood of Christ, and renew the creature, and set forth the image, and create inhabitants for the world above, aye, and, greatest of all, be God, and make others to be God? (2.72–73)

Gregory, realistic about the enormity of the pastoral task, feared being cast out, bound hand and feet, from the presence of Christ for having rashly entered into the lives of God's people (2.77). The church has wisely and long imposed a canonical age requirement for ordination. The deeper question, however, is the consideration of the maturity—theological, spiritual, and moral—of those who present themselves with ostensible calls to pastoral ministry.

Gregory hardly finds it helpful when he looks at the state of the priesthood in his own day. His words are harsh in criticism.

All fear has been banished from souls, shamelessness has taken its place, and knowledge and the deep things of the Spirit are at the disposal of anyone who will; and we all become pious by simply condemning the impiety of others; and we claim the services of ungodly judges, and fling that which is holy to the dogs, and cast pearls before swine, by publishing divine things in the hearing of profane souls, and, wretches that we are, carefully fulfil the prayers of our enemies, and are not even ashamed to go a whoring with our own inventions. . . . We observe each other's sins, not to bewail them, but to make them subjects of reproach, not to heal them, but to aggravate them, and excuse our own evil deeds by the wounds of our neighbours. (2.79–80)

Regarding the pastoral ministry, he charges, everything is in chaos, as priests fight over trivia with faith as the pretext, making the church a laughingstock as they contend for Christ in an un-Christlike manner (2.81–85).

Amid the moral, spiritual, and theological confusion among the clergy of his day, Gregory, as if to remind himself, asserts, "I have one remedy for them all, one road to victory: I will glory in Christ—namely, death for Christ's sake" (2.87). Yet in private, he too battles against the wiles of the wicked one, needing an armory with which to fight. "I own that I am too weak for this warfare, and therefore turned my back, hiding my face in the rout, and sat solitary, because I was filled with bitterness" (2.90). Even so, he remarks, "I have said nothing yet of the internal warfare within ourselves, and in our passions, in which we are engaged night and day against the body of our humiliation" (2.91). The point is as follows: It is not safe to entrust the care and cure of souls to a person who has not drawn close to God at the point of the real issues of personal life and been deeply converted through relationship with Christ.

Since then I knew these things, and that no one is worthy of the mightiness of God, and the sacrifice, and priesthood, who has not first presented himself to God, a living, holy sacrifice, and set forth the reasonable, well-pleasing service, and sacrificed to God the sacrifice of praise and the contrite spirit, which is the only sacrifice required of us by the Giver of all; how could I dare to offer to Him the external sacrifice, the antitype of the great mysteries, or clothe myself with the garb and name of priest, before my hands has been consecrated by holy works; before my eyes had been accustomed to gaze safely upon created things, with wonder only for the Creator, and without injury to the creature; before my ear has been sufficiently opened to the instruction of the Lord, and He had opened mine ear to hear without heaviness, and had set a golden earring with precious sardius, that is, a wise man's word in an obedient ear; before my mouth had been opened to draw in the Spirit, and opened wide to be filled with the spirit of speaking mysteries and doctrines; and my lips bound, to use the words of wisdom, by divine knowledge, and, as I would add, loosed in due season: before my tongue had been filled with exultation, and become an instrument of Divine melody, awaking with glory, awaking right early, and laboring till it cleave to my jaws: before my feet had been set upon the rock, made like hart's feet, and my footsteps directed in a godly fashion so that they should not well-nigh slip, nor slip at all; before all my members had become instruments of righteousness, and all mortality had been put off, and swallowed up life, and had yielded to the Spirit? (2.95)

Gregory's spiritual honesty makes for hard reading, for he demands an extraordinary level of repentance, amendment of life, and constant spiritual and moral vigilance from would-be pastors. "Who is the man?" Gregory cries repeatedly. That no one is spiritually worthy, and certainly not he, is the reason for his flight, and which, at the last, only obedience to the call of God can overcome. But before we jump too quickly to obedience, let us stay with Gregory here for a moment longer, for he holds up the danger of ministry. Ministry "is of all things most to be feared, this is the extremest of dangers in the eyes of everyone who understands that magnitude of success, the utter ruin of failure" (2.99). What Gregory has done, metaphorically speaking, is place a "spiritual health warning" over every candidate for holy orders. Gregory is at one with the classical tradition in pastoral theology in his recognition that God will hold pastors accountable for the souls given into their care (2.113). He has given aspiring pastors every reason to resist call until only obedience to an overwhelming demand is sufficient reason for advance to ministry.

Call and Obedience and the Place
of Spiritual Autobiography in Preparation for Ministry

While he did not want to be a pastor, in the end Gregory yielded to the duty of obedience. He did so even as he acknowledged that being an ordinary person and being faithful as such is better than risking the great gain of ministry (2.100). Nevertheless, Gregory took the high road and returned home from his flight for three reasons: a longing for his friends and brothers, responsibility for his aging parents, and most important of all, obedience to God's call. Drawing a lesson from the story of Jonah, Gregory observes that

> for God alone of all things cannot be escaped from or contended with; if He wills to seize and bring them under his hand, He outstrips the swift, He outwits the wise, He overthrows the strong, He abases the lofty, He subdues rashness, He represses power. (2.108)

About himself, he admits the fact that God had laid the yoke of ministry upon him, and that only fear of disobedience to God overcame his fear of failure in ministry (2.112). "Against the danger of disobedience I know of nothing which can help us, and of no ground to encourage our confidence" (2.113). Thus, repenting of his flight and becoming humble before the call of God, Gregory returned, recognizing that "I am commissioned to exalt Him in the congregation of the people, and praise Him in the seat of the elders" (2.115).

Why did Gregory cast his defense in part as a spiritual autobiography in the form of a public oration? The simple answer seems to be that the reasons for his flight and return lie deeply within the struggle of his own soul with God, and that an honest accounting for his actions required a telling of this struggle. The account, then, is of his struggle to identify and be obedient to his duty to God amidst his resistance to his call to ministry. The first word is "I." What follows is the report of his theological, spiritual, and moral debate with God, the God who cannot be escaped from or contended with, as Gregory maneuvers his way through the obstacles to priesthood placed in the way by his humanity. As the American Antiochian priest Fr. Joseph Allen helpfully notes, Gregory is concerned with discerning and coming to terms with his "priestly consciousness" (*hieratiki syneithesis*).[26] His treatise is also the account of his debate with the church, for the call to pastoral office is not a private affair, but belongs to the community. He wrote for both the congregation and himself. Ministry has a private and a public face, private and public accountability, and one of its most remarkable features is the seriousness of the task. Gregory allows his inquiry to pose questions concerning pastoral work that are profoundly challenging and disturbing and that en route teach the congregation the seriousness and complexity of the priestly office. He allows for no easy answers, for "we are far too low to perform the priest's office before God, and that we can only be worthy of the sanctuary after we have become worthy of the Church" (2.111). Neither is he impressed with or encouraged by what he saw of the priesthood: "I was ashamed of all those others, who, without being better than ordinary people . . . intrude into the most sacred offices. . . . They push and thrust around the holy table" (2.8).

Gregory would teach us thus: The responsibility of pastoral office is great indeed, and no one ought to enter who has not deeply examined motive and ability, who has not struggled against call in the face of the godly demands of office and the frailty of mere humanity, and for whom obedience alone is the yield of faithfulness. Self-knowledge is part of faithful preparation for ministry, but not only a knowledge of oneself in terms of immediate cultural, social, and familial contexts. The integration of one's personal story into the larger story of God's mission and call entails a purifying awareness of grace and sin that means a reckoning with Jesus Christ and his Gospel. Gregory's spiritual and theological introspection is a sanctifying and maturing process that matches the high demands of pastoral calling.

APPENDIX: AN OUTLINE OF "THE FLIGHT TO PONTUS"

The text of Gregory's "Flight to Pontus" is at times difficult to follow, and an English translation may be hard to find. The following summary is an overview of his argument.[27]

I. Introduction (1)

> Returned in submission to God.
> He intends to give reasons for his flight and return.
> He wants to explain his cowardice in order not to be a stumbling block to the community (2).

II. The Priesthood

> God has ordained order in the Body: some are to be subject to pastoral rule, others are to be pastors in order to perfect the church (3).
> Pastors function as the soul in the body and should surpass the majority in virtue and nearness to God.
> Anarchy and disorder are not godly (4).
> We need pastors for there must be leadership in the church and proper care given to worship and the sacraments.
> Pastors are more naturally those who are students of divine things (5).

III. Why Did He Run Away?

A. He was startled by the suddenness of ordination (6).

B. He longed for the contemplative life (6, 7).

C. He was embarrassed by the lifestyles of other priests who treat the priesthood as a livelihood and not as a vocation (8).

D. Most important, he was concerned over his own lack of qualifications to have authority over the souls of others (9).

> 1. A priest needs to be free from evil.
> In order to rule, a priest's own life must be impeccable. The more influence one has over others, the greater is the damage to others from one's own impurity (10). A rotten apple spoils the bunch.

Virtue is difficult to impart (11, 12). He is afraid of being a poor model for others (13).

2. A priest needs not only to be free from evil, but eminent in goodness (14).

   A priest needs to live by a higher standard so that he can draw people by the influence of persuasion, i.e., with gentleness, not by oppression and force (15).

3. The priest is a physician of souls (16).
   The guiding of others, the most variable of creatures, is the art of arts and the science of sciences. As such, pastoral care is difficult and challenging. The soul has the jobs (a) of wrestling with things below to make good our own choice and will; and (b) of freeing the body from its grossness so that body and soul together are fellow servants of God (17). [Gregory now moves to develop the work of the pastor similarly, as wrestling and freeing]

   Being a physician of souls involves:
   a. Wrestling, including the diagnosis and cure of our habits, passions, etc. (18), working with recalcitrant parishioners who wage an armed resistance against the pastor (19), and who hide away their sin or make excuses for it and are obstinate in hearing the truth or brazen it out (20). The battle is with the hidden heart of humankind and the adversary within (21).
   b. Freeing: the goal. The goal is to provide the soul with wings (22). This is the same goal held in the law and the prophets, and by Jesus and God (23, 24, 25). Pastors are fellow laborers with God for the healing of the people (26). The salvation of a soul is at stake (28).

   This work demands great skill, since people are so varied, and requires care correspondingly (28–33).

   Thus, the pastor must keep careful balance and guide people in a manner appropriate to their needs and nature, and worthy of the true Shepherd (34).

4. The priest must distribute the word (35). This is the first of all duties. The Word of God must regulate all that the priest does. Correct doctrine is vital (36). Discussion on the doctrine of the Trinity follows (37, 38). There are difficulties in discussing doctrine because of different approaches to understanding, speech, and hearing (39). Contending on behalf of God, the priest runs into problems against those who are fervent in faith but wrongheaded (40), who are arrogant towards or ignorant about correct teaching (41), who are stupid and fight against doctrine (41), or who are open to everything (42). Thus, working with people who are misinformed concerning

doctrine is very difficult (43). A teacher of the Word of God should then be straightforward, yet with a varied style in order to adapt to different audiences (44). Some people need to be fed with milk, while others require wisdom (45). Who, then, is sufficient? We must not distort the truth or dilute it in order to curry favor (46). Inexperienced as he, Gregory, is, it is folly to practice ministry before he is ready (47). How wise the Hebrew tradition was to appreciate that some scripture is to be left for one's older age (48). We are still spiritually immature but think ourselves wise (49). Evil indeed it is to try to teach others when we are not even aware of our own ignorance (50).

E. The witness of scripture is impressive regarding the importance of pastoral care and the seriousness with which pastors must take their work (51).

    1. Paul is the proof of the case concerning the care of souls (52–56).

    2. So also the prophets (56).

       a. Hosea (57).

       b. Micah (58).

       c. Joel (59).

       d. Habakkuk (60).

       e. Malachi (61).

       f. Zechariah (62, 63).

       g. Ezekiel (64–66).

       h. Jeremiah (67, 68).

    3. Paul's standards are high (69).

    4. Likewise, the standards of Jesus (69). What if we pastors merit his judgment? (70)

F. The burden of these thoughts (71). The truth is that the pastor must be godly before attempting to minister to others. It is not wise to take counsel from friends who lack reverence. It takes much time and experience to be ready to minister (72, 73). The truth is, God is beyond our knowing (74–76). Yet in fact Gregory declares he had been called to ministry from his youth, and his passions have been moderated (77). Even so, he was called to ministry before he felt he was ready.

G. Present problems:

    1. Unfaithful priests

       a. The priests treat the priesthood with contempt (78).

       b. They are shameless and ungodly in behavior (79).

       c. Others sins are used as an excuse (80).

d. Everything is in chaos and it cries out for solution (81).

e. People and pastors are equally bad off (82).

f. There is fighting over trivia in the name of faith (83).

g. The church is a laughingstock (84) as we contend for Christ in an un-Christlike manner (85). Thus Christ is blasphemed among unbelievers (86).

2. Satan

a. No matter the problem, Christ is the victory! (87)

b. Yet in things private, with what is one to be armed against the enemy? (88, 89)

c. Confession of weakness; all is shame (90).

d. To say nothing of internal warfare. Before we can minister to others we must overcome our own sin (91).

It is dangerous to stand before God when unfit.

I. The example of Moses (92);

II. Other OT examples (93).

III. The requirements of perfection in the Levitical priesthood (94).

H. Since no one is worthy, how can one offer oneself for ministry? (95) Who is the man

1. whose heart has not burned with the Word of God and attained the mind of Christ; (96)

2. who has not beheld the Lord, or passed over from law to grace; (97)

3. who has not contemplated the names of Christ or held communion with the word; (98)

4. who has not learned the hidden wisdom of God nor enrolled in the army of God; (99)

5. who will accept his appointment as head of the fullness of Christ? No one, if he will listen to me! (99) Ministry is DANGEROUS! (Emphasis added to indicate the strength of Gregory's warning.)

I. Summary of his flight. Better to be an ordinary person and do it well than to risk the great gain of ministry (100). Then the burdens are lighter and the punishments for failure less severe (101). Such is the defense; such are the reasons for the flight.

IV. Why Did He Return?

1. Longing for his friends and brothers (102).

2. Responsibility to his aging parents (103).

3. Of highest importance (104):

   a. The application of the story of Jonah (105–109)

   b. Jonah may have an excuse, but the yoke of ministry had been laid upon him (110).

   c. God's command, yet he felt torn between fear of unworthiness and the fear of disobedience, at last yielding to the latter (111–112).

   d. God certainly rewards our obedience, but against the danger of disobedience there is no solution (113).

   e. God is merciful to our wavering—OT examples (114).

   f. Thus, he repented, became humble before God, and returned (115).

V. Conclusion

   1. Here I am; give me your blessing (116).

   2. Prayer for God's guidance (117).

2

John Chrysostom
Six Books on the Priesthood

Anyone entrusted with men, the rational flock of Christ, risks a penalty not of money, but of his own soul for the loss of the sheep.

(II.2)

The shepherd needs great wisdom and a thousand eyes to examine the soul's condition from every angle.

(II.4)

I am afraid that if I receive the flock of Christ plump and well-fed and then damage it through ineptitude I may provoke against me God who so loved it that he gave himself for its salvation.

(II.4)

"Obey them that have the rule over you and submit to them; for they watch in behalf of your souls, as they that shall give account" (Hebrews 13:17). Is the fear of this threat trivial? We dare not say it is.

(III.18)

The fear of this threat continually disturbs my spirit.

(VI.1)

John, Bishop of Antioch and then of Constantinople, ranks not only as the foremost preacher of the Greek Church, but also as a pastor of the highest reputation. He was a simple and impulsive man, perhaps even naïve in the ways of the world, the one who lacked sometimes prudent judgment in

---

* St. John Chrysostom, *Six Books on the Priesthood*, trans. Graham Neville (Crestwood, N.Y.: St. Vladimir's Seminary Press, 1984).

public affairs, yet applied the highest standards of personal accountability to himself and to pastors. He was by all accounts a stern but good man, who, while fired by unyielding integrity, had a catholic disposition. He could be at once uncompromising in his demands upon himself and people in his pastoral and ecclesiastical charge, while welcoming monks fleeing persecution whose theology was less than correct. Unambiguously committed to Nicene orthodoxy, "he preached morals rather than dogmas, Christianity rather than theology, active, practical Christianity that proves itself in holy living and dying."[1] His predilections were ascetic and ethical rather than speculative, an Antiochene by birth and disposition. He was a man who attracted extremes of both loyalty and opposition.

John was about twenty years younger than Gregory of Nazianzus, and in February 398, John succeeded to Gregory's see at Constantinople. If they had direct contact, no record of it exists.[2] Less speculatively, we can assert that John's *Six Books on the Priesthood* shows the influence of Gregory's "Flight to Pontus," and, therefore, we see developing the great tradition in pastoral theology that nearly two hundred years later would extend into the West through Gregory the Great.

JOHN CHRYSOSTOM: A BRIEF BIOGRAPHY

As a mature man, John was not imposing. He was small in stature, with a body wasted from ascetic living. Two years of standing upright during his monastic period had permanently damaged his digestive system. He was described as being as frail as a spider's web. He had a large, bald head; a lofty, wrinkled forehead; deep-set, piercing eyes; and a prominent nose. His skin was pallid, his cheeks hollow, his ears large. He wore a sparse gray beard and, frequently, a severe expression.[3] He looked as he lived. His family name now long lost, he was nicknamed "Chrysostom" or "Golden Mouth" during the sixth century in recognition of his power with the spoken word.

The family was probably quite well off and well placed socially.[4] His father, Secundus, a senior civil servant, may have been of Roman descent. Secundus was not a Christian and died when John was an infant. His mother, Anthusa, widowed at age twenty, had a remarkable influence on her son, devoting herself to his formation and education. Historian Philip Schaff has written, "she shines with Noona and Monica among the most pious mothers of the fourth century, who prove the ennobling influence of Christianity on the character of women, and through her on all the family relations. . . . The famous advocate of heathenism, Lilanius, on hearing of her consistency and devotion, felt constrained to exclaim: 'Bless me! What wonderful women there are among the Christians.'"[5]

John was born in the middle of the fourth century,[6] into the political, theological, and ecclesiastical turbulence of Antioch. As a fourteen-year-old, he must have shared in the Christians' celebration of the sudden death of the militant pagan Emperor Julian, and heard the shout of "God and his Christ have triumphed."[7] His economic and social rank meant he would have been well schooled in the classical Greco-Roman curriculum of his day. Later, he studied rhetoric and philosophy under Libanius, the erudite and conservative pagan professor. He was a young man with great intellectual promise, probably training with an eye to government service. He was quick-tempered and self-assertive.[8] When Libanius was asked later whom he would have liked to have succeeded him, he replied: "John, if only the Christians had not stolen him from us."[9] According to John's early biographer, Palladius, John attached himself to Meletius, the orthodox bishop of Antioch who, attracted by the beauty of John's character, encouraged him to be continually in his company.[10] By then twenty-three years old, John offered himself for baptism. His baptism was the pivotal moment in his life, entailing for him a renunciation of the world and a dedication to the service of Christ.

Basil, John's interlocutory conversation partner in the rhetorical dialogue form of *Six Books on the Priesthood*, apparently was his encourager, luring him from the law courts and the theater, and from a life focusing on worldly desires and youthful vanities (37; I.3). With Basil he decided to turn to a life of solitude and the study of "the true philosophy," and together they considered establishing a monastic retreat. John's widowed mother, however, had other ideas. In an intimate, apparently autobiographical section in *Six Books on the Priesthood*, John tells at length of his mother's resistance to his plan, and of her need to have her only son at home. His mother recounts the difficulties of raising a son and of her fears of "a second bereavement," making her in effect a widow once again. Yielding to his mother's entreaties, he remained at home, turning his home into a monastery and living a simple, ascetic life of study and prayer. A good friend, a pious mother, and an able bishop together shaped the direction of John's life.

During this period, 370–374, the events recounted in the *Six Books on the Priesthood* took place, although the book itself was not written until the end of that decade, and, perhaps the beginning of the next.

After his mother's death, John retired to the deserted mountains south of Antioch, where he spent six years as a monk. According to one historian, "he retired to a cave, denied himself sleep, read the Bible continually, and spent two years without lying down, apparently in the belief that a Christian must stand in order to obey the injunction: "Be ye watchful." The result was inevitable: His stomach shriveled up, and his kidneys were damaged by cold. His digestion permanently impaired, unable to doctor himself, he came down from the mountain, walked to Antioch, and appeared before Archbishop Meletius, who immediately sent him to a doctor.[11] Excessive asceticism, then, brought his monastic years to an end, and for the sake of his health he returned to Antioch in 381. He was immediately ordained a deacon and, in 386, a priest. The account of his ostensible resistance to ordination is given in *Six Books on the Priesthood*. Whether the account has any factual basis in history remains unclear, for it may just be a rhetorical literary device to illustrate the seriousness of becoming a priest.

The church in Antioch, as indeed the church in general throughout the fourth century, was divided by deep theological debates. Theological tensions—pro and con the Nicene declaration on the relation of the Son to the Father—marked the life of the church of the day, and continued long after John's death. Preaching week by week, he was fearless in his exposition of the demands of Christian living in the face of the theological, moral, and political issues of the day—too fearless, perhaps, in his denunciations, for more gentle rebukes might have produced a better effect. He was a favorite of the crowds, yet he also aroused resentment among people who felt the sting of his oratorical powers.

One sermon from John's preaching during this period will illustrate the point. During Lent 387, facing the Emperor's threatened destruction of the city in reprisal for revolt against excessive taxation, John preached his twenty-one *Homilies on the Statues*—named for the toppling of the statues of the Emperor by the insurrecting crowds. In the midst of this terrible political crisis and violence, John worked his way through the prescribed Lectionary texts (on Genesis) to set the crisis in biblical perspective. But he also took the opportunity to preach against the ostentatious wealth of the rich, in comparison with poverty borne with humble spirit, and against the wickedness of the gossips, the evil lure of the theater, and the swearing of oaths. These Lenten sermons confirmed John as Antioch's premier preacher.

John's promotion to become bishop of Constantinople in 398 was, almost certainly, a surprise to him, although not necessary unwelcomed by him.[12] The city was the permanent seat of the Eastern emperor and a premier see of the Eastern Church. John's preaching and pastoral work soon attracted the attention of the Emperor Arcadius, a weak man, and his powerful wife, Eudoxia, who was to become an adversary. Invested heavily in his pastoral ministry, John declined to play the role of the court pastor. His moral sensibilities, his obstinacy, and his fierce integrity gained him enemies as he continued his attacks on vice, extravagance, and self-ishness. People whose feathers he ruffled called him "choleric." Others thought him "haughty." His biographer Palladius admits, "he did not trouble himself to be agreeable to any chance person."[13] Notably, also, he was unstinting in his criticism of the lax morals of the priests. His sense of the gospel missionary imperative led him to a remarkable pastoral min-istry to the numerous Goths in the capital city, having part of the Bible translated for them and preaching to them through an interpreter.

The events that led to his downfall and exiles have to do with the resent-ment and enmity of the empress and Theophilus, bishop of Alexandria, who had reluctantly consecrated him. First, in 401 John traveled to Eph-esus, intervening on behalf of clergy there, deposing six bishops on the charge of simony. During his absence, the empress began to organize to depose the bishop. Then, on his return, John referred to Elijah's relation to Jezebel in an obvious reference to the empress. She took the reference, as he intended, as a personal insult.

Second, John became involved in the defense of some fifty Origenist monks (members of a heretical group) whom Theophilus had expelled, but who John received. Theophilus himself sailed to Constantinople as John's accuser and judge, and with the empress and the disaffected clergy in atten-dance laid charges against him. The so-called Synod at the Oak (403) met, banishing John from the city into exile on twenty-nine trumped-up charges. A spontaneous riot in support of the bishop resulted, with the people chanting before the palace gates, "Give us back our bishop!" Yet nature, not politics, turned the tide. The night after John's deposition, a violent earthquake shook the city, bringing even the empress to repen-tance. John was hastily summoned back to enter the city in triumph.

The rapprochement between the bishop and the empress did not endure. Vain and imperious, she had erected a statue of herself for public adoration outside the Church of Hagia Sophia. While documentation is uncertain, John was reported to have said, preaching on the Feast of St. John the Baptist: "Again Herodias is raging, again she is dancing, again she demands the head of John the Baptist on a platter."[14] This allusion was an unforgivable insult, as far as the empress was concerned. She demanded a response from her husband. During the baptismal rite on the Vigil of the Resurrection, Imperial guards dragged John from his cathedral. On June 5, 404, John was deposed and banished to Cucusus, in the mountains of Armenia—he called it a "lost corner of the world"[15]—from whence he received visitors and engaged in lively correspondence. The empress, not yet content with John's plight, ordered him once more removed to Pityus, a truly inhospitable place. Feeble, old, and sick, he died en route on Saturday, September 14, 407, as his guards forced him ever deeper into exile. At his final Communion that day he is recorded to have said again his habitual doxology, "Glory to God for all things, Amen."

John's life was in many ways a tragedy, yet his moral character and strength of spiritual and theological conviction mark him as one of the most important Fathers of the fourth century. While not in the strict sense a martyr, he died for his faith.[16]

THEMES IN JOHN'S THEOLOGY

John was not a theologian in a formal sense, but was rather a pastor and preacher whose ministry was deeply rooted in the plain meaning of scripture and the orthodoxy of Nicene theology interpreted in the light of Antiochian Christology. We will look briefly at these two topics in the context of the distinction that is sometimes offered between Alexandrian and Antiochian approaches.[17]

Alexandrian versus Antiochene Exegesis[18]

Surveying the approach to scripture found in eight Fathers of the fourth, fifth, and sixth centuries, the historian of doctrine Christopher Hall concludes: "All agreed that personal disposition and spiritual health affect one's ability to read scripture well. All agreed that once the exegete has determined the meaning of the biblical text and plumbed its possible applications, the text's inherent divine authority summons the biblical interpreter to obedience. All agreed that biblical interpretation is a Christian communal endeavor the exegete must practice within the context of Christ's body, the church."[19] The Fathers also saw that the grammatical-historical meaning of a biblical passage, its plain or literal meaning, was not the end of the interpretation. Layers of meaning were to be expected. They differed though in the way they understood how this spiritual meaning was to be uncovered and reported.[20] While driving too aggressively a wedge between the Alexandrian and Antiochene schools is inappropriate, they certainly had distinct and different emphases.

The Alexandrian school, heavily influenced in this regard by Origen and Philo, was motivated at least in part by an apologetic concern: How was the Bible to be communicated to the Greek world? Given the need always to do historico-grammatical exegesis first of all, some observers believe that allegorical or symbolic interpretation developed as a way around the problems raised by the literalism of many biblical stories. According to Schaff (who is unsympathetic towards this approach), as a hermeneutical method such interpretation is impositional rather than expositional, reading into the text what is not appropriate.[21] For that reason allegory must be used only rarely and with great control. What Christian preacher has not interpreted the major parables of Jesus or the significant narratives of Hebrew history in an allegorical manner, often with outrageous results that are a long way from the plain meaning of the text? The dangers of allegory are self-evident, for they can lead away from the meaning of a text. Interpreters must beware lest the interpretation has more to do with their imaginations and the exigencies of the homiletical moment than with the meaning of the text itself.

The English patristic scholar Andrew Louth has argued, however, for a more sympathetic interpretation of allegorical interpretation. For the Fathers, according to Louth, allegorical interpretation "was not a superfluous, stylistic habit, something we can fairly easily lop off from the trunk of patristic theology. Rather it is bound up with their whole understanding of tradition as the tacit dimension of the Christian life: allegory is a way of entering the 'margin of silence' that surrounds the articulate message of the scriptures, it is a way of glimpsing the living depths of tradition."[22] The use of allegory, then, is not intended to discount the plain meaning of the text, but to listen across a history that is filled with tradition. What unites us with the writers of scripture, after all, is the Church,[23] so any severe distinction between scripture and tradition is really nonsensical. Tradition is the cradle within which scripture is both received and read. Allegorical sensitivity in the exposition of a biblical text amounts to the awareness of multiple layers of meaning in a text. It is, says Louth, "a way of holding us before the mystery which is the ultimate 'difficulty' of the Scriptures."[24] For the Fathers, allegorical interpretation was a way of honoring the mystery to which the scriptures bear witness.

A rival tradition developed at Antioch, which is more in accord with modern and Protestant sensibilities,[25] and of which John Chrysostom is the best-known representative. The Antiochene school came into its own with Chrysostom's teacher, Diodore of Tarsus (d. 393) and further developed under Chrysostom and his colleague Theodore of Mopsuestia (d. 429). The hermeneutical theories of the Antiochene school were clearly aimed at ameliorating the excesses of Alexandrian allegorical exegesis and spirituality.[26]

In a manner similar to the Alexandrian school, Diodore advanced the view that the biblical exegete must develop an interpretative disposition, an appropriate attitude or cast of mind, that identifies the spiritual meaning lying embedded within the historical framework.[27] The attempt to reach a spiritual reading of the text, however, he argued, must always be subject to the indispensable historical kernel that anchors the text in empirical reality; to fail to do so leads to an inappropriate allegorical reading. Theodore of Mopsuestia makes the theological observation that searching for the meaning of a text beyond history threatens the gospel itself.[28] The Antiochene tradition, then, looked for the plain grammatical and historical sense of a text, drawing from the word what is actually there.

Quasten sums up and judges John Chrysostom's approach in this way:

> Most of (his) sermons were delivered at Antioch between 386 and 397. They give evidence of his strict and intelligent training in the tenets of that School. Always anxious to ascertain the literal sense and opposed to allegory, he combines great facility in discerning the spiritual meaning of the Scriptural text with an equal ability for immediate, practical application to the guidance of those committed to his care. The depth of his thought and the soundness of his masterful exposition are unique and attract even modern readers. He is equally at home in the books of the Old and the New Testament and has the skill to use even the former for the conditions of the present and the problems of daily life.[29]

Chrysostom adopted a matter-of-fact approach to scripture, placing himself into the contexts of the texts themselves by understanding the ordinary use of language. From this vantage point he derived spiritual meanings and applications, making them "useful for teaching, for reproof, for correction, and for training in righteousness, so that everyone who belongs to God may be proficient, equipped for every good work" (2 Tim. 3:16–17). To take just one example: in his Third Homily on the Gospel According to St. Matthew, and the third sermon on the text of verse one, he gives his reasons for so long a discussion. It is necessary, he states, to probe into aspects of the text that are "more mystical and secret" than those discussed in the previous homilies. Following a discussion of the lineage of Jesus and the meaning of the role of Joseph, Chrysostom moves to a discussion of haughtiness and pride, and of the need for self-restraint. "Let us with great diligence implant in our souls the mother of all things that are good, I mean humility."[30] His move from historical exegesis to moral application is evident as he develops the spiritual significance of the first verse of the Gospel According to Saint Matthew.

Chrysostom's Antiochene Christology

Chrysostom's life and theology represented an inseparable whole.[31] The teaching and the man were congruent: orthodox, practical, pastoral. As did his exegetical method, his Christology favored the school of Antioch. A preacher and pastor rather than a theologian who apprehended and developed the faith in new ways, he was a supporter without qualification of Nicene theology, but with an Antiochene emphasis on the humanity of Jesus. His orthodoxy is expressed thus:

> Remaining what He was, He assumed what He was not, and though He became man, remained God, in that He was the Word. . . . He became the one (man), He took the one (man). He was the other (God). Thus there is no confusion, but also no separation. One God, one Christ, the Son of God. But when I say one (Christ), I mean thereby a union and not a commingling, not that one nature is trans-muted into another, but is united to that other.[32]

How is this union possible? His reply: Do not ask.

In contrast to Alexandrian Christology, with its Athanasian soteriolog-ical emphasis, and in contrast to his later contemporary Augustine in the West, Chrysostom adopted a kind of unofficial semi-Pelagianism. He stressed free will, a cause surely of his sense of moral urgency and of human cooperation with the grace of God. Little trace appears of the language and conceptual apparatus of later Augustianism and Protestantism: no doctrines of absolute predestination, depravity, hereditary guilt, irresistible grace, forensic justification. According to Philip Schaff: "He teaches that God foreordained all men to holiness and salvation, and that Christ died for all and is both willing and able to save all, but not against their will and without their free consent. . . . The will of man, though injured by the Fall, has still the power to accept or to reject the offer of salvation. It must first obey the divine call."[33] While faith and good works appear to be necessary conditions for salvation, Christ alone is the efficient cause, whose merits are adequate to draw all people to the Father. Contemporary Pietism would most likely find in John Chrysostom a theological soul mate, a preacher who even for our time can serve as a contrast to the rigorous theology of total grace in expressions of neoorthodoxy.

One final point must be noted: Chrysostom taught a doctrine of the real presence of Christ in the Eucharist. He would have the approach to the Eucharist be with awe and devotion, and with a sense of the holy mys-tery that there confronts us.[34] Christ there is truly present under the ele-ments of bread and wine. Thus in a sermon on Matthew, he says, pointing to the altar, "Christ there lies slain." "That which is in the chalice is the same as what flowed from the side of Christ. What is the bread? The Body of Christ." And again: "How many people say today: I would like to see Him, Himself, His face, His features, His clothes, His shoes! Well, you see Him, you touch Him, you eat Him. . . . He gives Himself to you."[35] Even the priest, at the moment of consecration, is Christ himself: "Believe that there takes place now the same banquet as that in which Christ sat at table. . . . It is not man who causes what is present to become the Body and Blood of Christ, but Christ Himself who was crucified for us."[36]

For his teaching on the Eucharist, John Chrysostom has been called the *doctor eucharisticus* of the Eastern Church. He is also a Doctor of the Church, a man who as priest and preacher, as churchman and moral leader, lived what he taught with integrity and intensity to embody the Gospel of Jesus Christ amid the extraordinary political, theological, and ecclesiastical complexities of his time. In the context of his life and teaching, and not in any disembodied sense, should the *Six Books on the Priesthood* be read, interpreted, and, where appropriate, applied in the life of the Church today. While he remains a person of his time, John Chrysostom is still, even for non-Orthodox Western Protestants, a Doctor of the Church, a teacher of Christian faith accorded the highest status by those who have followed him.

THE PASTORAL THEOLOGY
OF JOHN CHRYSOSTOM

John Chrysostom wrote the *Six Books on the Priesthood* between 380 and 386, during his diaconate in Antioch, shortly after he abandoned his monastic life. The work was written first of all to instruct the church on the reform of the practice of the ministry by increasing the understanding of the importance, responsibilities, and difficulties of the pastoral office.[37] Only secondarily did he write a personal defense against criticism of his craven action whereby his friend Basil was tricked into being ordained by believing that Chrysostom had presented himself for ordination as well. Like Gregory of Nazianzus before him and Gregory the Great after him, Chrysostom sought to avoid or delay ordination, though in his case by a deceitful trick played against Basil. The treatise is both a discussion of the pastoral office and an explanation for his behavior. Focusing attention on the positive contribution that Chrysostom makes to literature on pastoral ministry is far more helpful for us than dwelling on the peculiar story of deceit and trickery that begins the treatise.

With respect to the practice of pastoral care today, three issues emerge from the text for our consideration: (1) the nature of the pastoral office, (2) the tasks and problems of preaching, and (3) the piety of the pastor.

The Nature of the Pastoral Office

For John Chrysostom, the ministry of the church is to be understood and practiced solely in terms of spiritual and theological criteria. This point should not be taken for granted, for easily pragmatic and functional criteria can be given prescriptive authority especially under pressures from pressing pastoral need. At the beginning of Book II he establishes his position with a decisive exegesis of the commissioning of Peter (John 21: 15–19).

> The Master asked the disciple if he loved him, not to learn the truth—why should he, who lives in all men's hearts?—but to teach us how much he cares for the supervision of these flocks. . . . He did not want to prove then how much Peter loved him (which was already clear to us from many pieces of evidence), but he wanted Peter and all of us to learn how much he loves his own Church, in order that we too might show great concern for the same thing. (52–53; II.1)

More than the call to a monastic or ascetic life, more than becoming a champion of the wronged or a father to the fatherless, Peter is called by Christ to "tend my sheep." Chrysostom wanted to drive home the cardinal point that the pastoral office is of the highest importance; that office also must be understood theologically first of all to be a sharing in Christ's own love for his people. Ministers are representatives of Christ, going about an employment very close to the Lord's heart. Thus, according to Chrysostom, only those who far exceed all others in spiritual excellence are fit for office. Further, so serious is the responsibility when Christ entrusts his church into the care of pastors, that "anyone entrusted with men, the rational flock of Christ, risks a penalty not of money, but of his own soul for the loss of the sheep" (54; II.2). Ministry, then, is an activity rooted at all points in the gospel; ministry is the fruit of a sanctified life, for the exercise of which pastors will be held accountable by God.

Chrysostom uses two arguments to emphasize the nature of the ministry given by Christ to pastors and to distinguish pastors from lay people, as well as to justify his refusal to be ordained a priest. These arguments go to excessive lengths to distinguish the pastoral office from the service of lay people.

First, he compares a pastor of the people to a shepherd of the sheep, but then almost immediately softens the comparison: "let the difference

between shepherd and sheep be as great as the distinction between rational and irrational creatures, not to say even more, since matters of much
greater moment are at stake" (54; II.2). Chrysostom is wise to have tempered this concept. Both the Bible and Christian tradition use rural and
agricultural images to describe the nature and tasks of ministry, but dangers lurk. Shepherds are human, sheep are animals. The relationship is
unequal at all points. Further, shepherds farm sheep in order to kill and
eat them. In an increasingly urban and suburban society, the use of
metaphorical shepherds is not a helpful device to illuminate the meaning
of ministry when most people have seen neither non-metaphorical shepherds or sheep. Perhaps aware of his extreme statement, Chrysostom
immediately shifts his use of the shepherd-sheep metaphor by observing
correctly that

> You cannot treat men with the same authority with which a shepherd
> treats a sheep.

And the reason?

> [I]t is necessary to make a man better not by force but by persuasion.
> We neither have authority granted us by law to restrain sinners, nor,
> if it were, should we know how to use it, since God gives the crown to
> those who are kept from evil, not by force, but by choice. (56; II.3)

The pastor is not a different kind of being from the people, and ministry does not proceed by coercion. Nevertheless, by using the figure of
the pastor as a shepherd Chrysostom has tried to make two points: (1) the
pastor must exercise solicitous care over the people that mirrors Christ's
own care for his church, and (2) he, John, believes himself unworthy of
the task. As we saw in the previous chapter, Gregory of Nazianzus also
expressed these points. The positive point is an enduring truth with regard
to ministry, especially when, as in Chrysostom's time, standards among
the clergy had grown lax.

Second, Chrysostom viewed the pastoral office in terms of metaphysical assumptions that come to light in his account of theological anthropology and ecclesiology.[38] He argued that the authority of a priest parallels
the relationship of soul to body. Again this parallels the theology of Gregory of Nazianzus. Physical existence is not evil, but assumes positive
value by being raised to a spiritual plane by the soul. As the soul is over
the body, so the priest is over the layperson. As the soul raises the body to
its spiritual level, so the priest raises the layperson. This ministry is ultimately controlled by the Eucharist, which is the "place" where heaven and
earth meet in order to take the human up to God. From the hands of the

priest in the Eucharist, God comes to earth. With this argument Chrysostom intended to show the ontological nature of the authority of the priest, the theoretical basis, we might say, of his program for the reform of the clergy.

Chrysostom, then, thought in terms of a hierarchical universe in which the spiritual is "above" the physical, and the soul "above" the body, and in which the spiritual confers meaning and value on the physical. He never implies that the body is evil or is the source of evil. Rather, he emphasizes that "heaven is more precious than earth and souls than bodies" (72; III.5). All the more interesting, then, is Chrysostom's well-known concern for the physical and material welfare of his people. In fact, his view of the body is largely positive. Nevertheless, he argues that spiritual blessedness is of singular importance and especially so in regard to the understanding and tasks of pastoral ministry, for great indeed is the battle that takes place in the spiritual realm. After a lurid description of physical battle on land and warfare at sea, he writes:

> If it were possible to strip off this body, or even to keep it on and see clearly and undismayed with the naked eye the devil's whole battle-line and the warfare he wages against us, you would see no torrents of blood, no dead bodies, but so many spiritual corpses and such horrible wounds that you would think all that picture of warfare which I have just described to you was mere child's play, and sport rather than war, so many there are every day who perish. (157; VI.13)

Earlier on in the treatise Chrysostom cited Ephesians 6:12 to similar effect[39] (55; II.2).

This approach does not mean that the church is to be understood solely in spiritual terms. The present inquiry, he writes,

> concerns the very Body of Jesus. For the Church of Christ is Christ's own Body, according to St. Paul, and the man who is entrusted with it must train it to perfect health and incredible beauty, by unremitting vigilance to prevent the slightest plot or wrinkle or other blemish of that sort from marring its grace and loveliness. In short, he must make it worthy, as far as lies within human power, of that pure and blessed Head to which it is subjected. (114; IV.2)

The church is the *body* of Christ. But it is subjected to its spiritual head, Jesus Christ, for from him comes its identity. Thus, physical existence, even for the church, has a place in the scheme of things, but orientation to the spiritual realm is finally important.

Chrysostom operates within a metaphysical hierarchy that places human beings, priests and then monks and virgins in ascending ontological order. The priest functions in a mediating position between the heavenly and physical realms.

> The work of the priesthood is done on earth, but it is ranked among heavenly ordinances. And this is only right, for no man, no angel, no archangel, no other created power, but the Paraclete himself ordained this succession, and persuaded men, while still remaining in the flesh, to represent the ministry of angels. The priest, therefore, must be as pure as if he were standing in heaven itself in the midst of those powers. (70; III.4)

The priest, as it were, brings heaven to earth and earth to heaven—so much so that God confirms in heaven, according to Chrysostom, what priests do on earth (72; III.5).

The sacrament of the Eucharist especially is the action in which the cosmos is finally defined and the role of the priest put into clearest perspective.

> For if a man "cannot enter into the kingdom of heaven except he be born again of water and the spirit," and if he that eateth not the Lord's flesh and drinketh not his blood is cast out of everlasting life, and all these things can happen through no other agency except their sacred hands (the priest's, I mean), how can anyone, without their help, escape the fire of Gehenna or win his appointed crown? They are the ones—they and no others—who are in charge of spiritual travail and responsible for the birth that comes through baptism. Through them we put on Christ and are united with the Son of God and become limbs obedient to that blessed Head. (73; III.5–6)

Without the benefit of a priest there can be no salvation!

I wish to make two observations. First, and positively, highlighting again the importance of the pastoral office for the salvation and spiritual well-being of persons is beneficial. God has ordained pastors, among others, to build up of the body of Christ.

> The gifts he gave were that some would be apostles, some prophets, some evangelists, some pastors and teachers, to equip the saints for the work of ministry, for building up the body of Christ. (Eph. 4:11–12)

Though not cited by Chrysostom, Romans 10:14–15 also remains critical for understanding and appreciating ministry:

> But how are they to call on one in whom they have not believed? And how are they to believe in one of whom they have never heard? And how are they to hear without someone to proclaim him? And how are they to proclaim him unless they are sent? As it is written, "How beautiful are the feet of those who bring good news!"

For our time, too, it is important to reaffirm the high calling of ministers to care for Christ's people in a manner that reflects Christ's love for them—which may not be the same as managing a congregation or forging a career! At a time when pastoral work does not carry high social status; when ministers on the whole are very poorly paid, have low professional self-esteem, and receive less and less job satisfaction, and yet tend to overwork; when the mainline Protestant churches are rife with conflict; and when received models of ministry appear to be breaking down, John Chrysostom reminds us of the truth: the pastoral vocation comes from the call of God. Indeed, pastoral work is built into the metaphysical structure of God's re-creation. Pastoral work has a God-given dignity and significance that no one and no church dare take away, and pastors themselves must carefully attend to and exercise this authority with appropriate diligence.

Second, and critically, however, Chrysostom's theological foundation is seriously, perhaps fatally, flawed for Protestants insofar as he replaces the priesthood of Christ with the priesthood of the pastor/priest. Christ, apparently, is ascended so far above creation that he, the mediator, needs a mediator to bring him down to earth again. His vicarious humanity—by which he became as we are that we might be joined to him and become by grace as he is by nature, to share in that which is his—has simply vanished into the heavens. Just this role of mediating the mediator has tended to be played by Mary, as well as the saints and priests in Roman Catholicism and Orthodoxy. Chrysostom's metaphysical order of being is unacceptable. What, however, should Protestantism today put in its place? Arguably, the major problem that pastoral theology faces today is not the lack of skills, or even the lack of piety, among the clergy but the lack of an adequate theological foundation for pastoral ministry by which they can understand their work to be profoundly rooted in God's redemptive and eschatological purpose. Chrysostom leaves us with a constructive theological task still to do that is as urgent for the renewal of ministry in our day as his task was in his.

The Tasks and Problems of Preaching and Teaching the Christian Faith

Pastoral work today tends to be construed in terms of face-to-face counseling, the consequence perhaps of an overreliance on psychology and psychotherapy. Having established its identity by way of the auxiliary discipline of psychology, pastoral care studies tend subsequently to be separated from the other disciplines in practical theology, homiletics, evangelism, and Christian education. John Chrysostom had a larger vision that was in essence a unified practical theology in which preaching, evangelism, and teaching have a central place in the care of souls. His reason for a unified view is basic: only sound teaching can heal sickness of soul (115; IV.3). Chrysostom was not an advocate of salvation through reason and argument; he recognized, rather, that if we think wrongly about God, we will live wrongly. Referring to the elders who labor in word and teaching (1 Tim. 5:17), Chrysostom remarks that their ultimate aim was "to lead their disciples, both by what they do and what they say, into the way of that blessed life which Christ commanded. Example alone is not sufficient instruction" (125; IV.8).

Chrysostom's ministry took place in a time of intense theological controversy, when the church was contending for the very existence of the Christian faith. In the face of heterodoxy, his was a time of establishing orthodoxy, and, in particular, central doctrines concerning the person of Jesus Christ and the Trinity. The issue that the church struggled to clarify, in other words, was the *Christian* doctrine of God. The ministry of the spoken word was, therefore, a primary weapon in the pastor's armory to defend the people against the spiritual attacks of false doctrine:

> no other help has been vouchsafed but that of the word. And if anyone is deprived of this power, the souls of those under him (I mean the weaker and more speculative of them) will not be better off than ships storm-tossed at sea. So the priest should do all he can to gain this power. (119; IV.5)

Today as well, ministry faces the challenge of an aggressive doctrinal heterodoxy. Mainline Protestantism finds itself again having to contend reductionist theological proposals for the central doctrines of Christian faith and the Christian apprehension of God. In this situation, pastors must accept the challenge to be teaching elders.

> [W]hen it is false doctrine that the soul is suffering from, words are urgently needed, not only for the safety of the Church's members, but to meet the attacks of outsiders as well. (115; IV.3)

This challenge demands, then as now, ability in public speaking. Even more so, the words demand theological perspicacity. According to Chrysostom,

> Let a man's diction be beggarly and his verbal composition simple and artless, but do not let him be inexpert in the knowledge and careful statement of doctrine. And do not let him deprive the saint, to cloak his own idleness, of the greatest of his qualities and the chief of his claims of eulogy. (121; IV.6)

For Chrysostom, then, one could not act faithfully as a pastor without teaching faithfully as a theologian. He understood the salutary implications of sound teaching, and the moral and spiritual dangers of its lack.

Above all else, Chrysostom was known as the "golden-mouthed" preacher. That he devoted about one third of his treatise to preaching and teaching is hardly surprising. What is remarkable about these pages is the seemingly autobiographical tenor of his admonitions to the preacher. Was he admonishing himself? Whatever the case, he is pungent in his comments and severe with his pen as he probes into the inner fears and delights of the preacher, which clearly is his main point. He is also merciless in his withering scorn for the foolishness of those who sit in the pews.

Chrysostom begins with two basic points. First, the sermon is the primary means for sowing the seed of faith. As he everywhere also maintains, sound teaching is also necessary for guarding the growth of faith. Second, people listen to the sermon in judgment, attending for pleasure, not profit (127; V.1). Thus,

> a man needs a loftiness of mind far beyond my own littleness of spirit, if he is to correct this disorderly and unprofitable delight of ordinary people, and to divert their attention to something more useful. (128; V.1)

Three virtues especially, he argued, must characterize the moral performance of the preacher: contempt of praise, force of eloquence, and a despising of slander and envy. Contempt of praise especially is vital for a preacher.

> What troubles and vexations do you suppose a man endures, if he enters the lists of preaching with this ambition for applause? (130; V.4)

Indeed,

> the man who has accepted the task of teaching should pay no attention to the commendation of outsiders, any more than he should let them cause him dejection. When he has composed his sermons to please God (and let this alone be his rule and standard of good oratory in sermons, not applause or commendation), then if he should be approved by men too, let him not spurn their praise. But if his hearers do not accord it, let him neither seek it or sorrow for it. It will be sufficient encouragement for his efforts, and one much better than anything else, if his conscience tells him he is organizing and regulating his teaching to please God. (133; V.7)

Without contempt for praise, no amount of excellent technique will ensure faithful preaching. Without contempt for praise, the preacher chooses merely to be an entertainer. And, he warns,

What awful disaster, what burning fire is heaped on that wretched man's head for every one of these souls that perish, you do not need me to tell you, since you know it perfectly well." (126; IV.9)

The preacher, Chrysostom notes, must also learn to overcome criticism, not by ignoring it, but by treating it at its source.

Then we shall not only strangle evil reports at birth and eradicate them, but even foresee their source far in advance, remove the pretexts from which they spring, and not wait for them to be established and bandied about on everyone's lips. (149; VI.9)

However, if criticism should gain the upper hand in a preacher's own mind, he or she should beware, "for despondency and constant anxieties have a terrible power to numb the soul and reduce it to utter impotence" (129: V.4). Thus Chrysostom counsels that a preacher should treat the congregation

as a father treats very young children. We are not disturbed by children's insults or blows or tears; nor do we think much of their laughter and approval. And so with these people, we should not be much elated by their praise nor much dejected by their censure. (129; V. 4)

And just when one might judge Chrysostom to be ignorant of family life and the pathos of being a parent as to render his analogy invalid, he poignantly observes: "This is not easy, my friend, and I think it may be impossible" (130; V.4).

Finally, deepening the moral complexities of preaching, Chrysostom discusses the congregation to whom one speaks: The preacher has to contend with their ignorance, partisanship, and boredom. How can anyone, he asks,

endure the deep disgrace of having his sermon received with blank silence and feelings of boredom, and his listeners waiting for the end of the sermon as if it were a relief after fatigue? . . . [I]t is enough to kill enthusiasm and paralyse spiritual energy. (135; V.8)

Further, he notes, preaching takes place, then as now, within the cauldron of theological controversy, and the preacher must be able to handle the tensions and complexities of debate:

[W]hen conflicts arise on matters of doctrine and all the combatants rely on the same scriptures, what weight will his life carry then? What use are a man's many labors, when after all his exertions he falls into heresy through sheer inexperience and is cut off from the body of Christ, as I know many have done? What help is his perseverance? None at all . . . That is the chief reason why anyone who has the responsibility of teaching others must be experienced in these doctrinal conflicts. For though he himself stands secure and is not injured by his opponents; yet, when the multitude of simpler folk who are set under him see their leader worsted and unable to answer his opponents, they do not blame his incapacity for the defeat, but his unsound doctrine. So through the inexperience of one man the whole congregation is brought to ultimate disaster. (125–6; IV.9)

In this light, preaching emerges as an ascetic discipline. Manuals and courses on preaching abound today, yet from Chrysostom, the greatest preacher of the Greek church, we learn a lesson only very rarely found elsewhere. A faithful preacher sports much more than sound rhetorical technique and a good theological education. Also required are an interior disposition of heart in which self-knowledge and a rigorous turning to God are very important. Evagrius Ponticus, an early father of the church, once observed that a theologian is a person whose prayer is true. We might paraphrase that and say that a preacher is a person whose prayer *and heart* are true. Faithfulness in preaching, says Chrysostom, comes not by nature, but by hard work and constant application in which the desire alone is to please God. And first of all, says Chrysostom, if we would do this, is the need to test our own soul (109; IV.1).

We turn finally in our review of the pastoral theology of John Chrysostom to the issue of the pastor's piety.

The Piety of the Pastor

Chrysostom's teaching on piety may be summed up as follows:

[T]he priest's soul must be purer than the rays of the sun, in order that the Holy Spirit may never leave him desolate, and that he may be able to say, "I live; yet no longer I, but Christ liveth in me." (137; VI.2)

The ministry, then, requires "angelic virtue" (137; VI.2). Whether this is hyperbole or perfectionism we shall have to decide. Not in dispute, however, is the seriousness with which Chrysostom takes the spiritual and moral formation of the pastor. He makes his reason clear throughout the treatise, but especially in Book VI where he expounds at length on the burden of worldly cares and attacks of the devil that beset a pastor, and in Book III where he deals with issues of character. Having to account to God for the care of those who are a pastor's responsibility, no excuse will be acceptable, neither ignorance nor inexperience. Chrysostom, then, treats his subject in two ways, concerned as he is with both external temptations and with internal dispositions of character.

> How much ability, then, and how much strength do you suppose the priest needs to enable him to keep his soul from every contamination and preserve its beauty unimpaired? . . . [H]e is prey to more temptations, which can defile him unless he makes his soul inaccessible to them by the practice of unremitting self-denial and strict self-discipline. (137; VI.2)

Nothing feeds the work of evil within us more successfully than our exposure to external temptations that we do not resist. Chrysostom cautions that pastors must watch out for the "extra fuel for the flame supplied by sight from the external world" (139; VI.3). In Book VI, Chrysostom twice uses the example of temptations by women to illustrate his point (147; VI.8 and 153: VI.12). These examples might suggest to some a misogynist tendency; on the other hand, and not ruling out misogyny, the texts suggest that he writes from his own experience of attraction to women. In view of our heightened awareness today of sexual harassment and sexual misbehavior by pastors, these remarks from the fourth century have contemporary resonance. Chrysostom's contribution is that he recognized the issue as more than a psychological but also as a moral concern. His point is, in any case, pastors "who lead their lives in the thick of things" (139: VI.3) are vulnerable to temptations, much more so than monastics who can hide themselves away from the world, and must therefore give virtue and prudence and an ascetic detachment the highest spiritual attention.

> A priest must not only be blameless, as befits one chosen for so high a ministry, but also very discreet and widely experienced. He ought to be as much aware of mundane matters as any who live in the midst of them, and yet be more detached from them than the monks who have taken to the mountains. (141; VI.4)

The trials of ministry test the souls of pastors. The ministry is dangerous work for the soul. Fundamentally, then, Chrysostom issues a call to purity in the midst of worldliness, and to a spirituality in which pastors pay highest attention to their own moral lives. He has two reasons for this call. First, the pastor has a responsibility to God:

> when he invokes the Holy Spirit and offers that awful sacrifice and keeps on touching the common Master of us all, tell me, where shall we rank him? What purity and what piety shall we demand of him? Consider how spotless should the hands be that administer these things, how holy the tongue that utters these words. Ought anyone to have a purer and holier soul than one who is to welcome this great Spirit? (140; VI.4)

Second, the pastor has a responsibility to the church and the people. So the pastor must work for the well-being of people, help them when burdened, and comfort them in the midst of many trials. Thus, "all these different methods look to one object: the glory of God and the edification of the Church" (142; VI.4).

Turning now to issues of character formation and personal affective dispositions, Chrysostom asks, "what about the man whose task is to adorn the bride of Christ? How much strength in himself and from above do you think he needs to avoid complete failure?" (75; III.7). "Everyone wants to judge the priest, not as one clothed in flesh, not as one possessing a human nature, but as an angel, exempt from the frailty of others" (86; III.14). In various places Chrysostom treats of vainglory ("more dangerous than the Sirens' rock") and ambition, sluggishness, anger, and temper. Blinded by inexperience in the things of their own spirits, pastors fill the congregations entrusted to them with 1,001 troubles (79; III.10).

In response, Chrysostom offers three areas that require a pastor's attention. First, a pastor must free himself or herself from ambition for office. Pastors must be "on our guard against ambition and examine ourselves carefully to prevent a spark of it from smouldering anywhere unseen" (81; III.11). Ambition is the doorway through which evil enters the spirit, for one will then do anything to seize the object of desire. Second, a pastor must be clear-sighted and sober, "for he lives, not for himself alone, but for a great multitude" (82; III.12). Third, a pastor must have spiritual strength to bear the hurts that come with the office without striking back. "A furious temper causes great disasters both to its possessor and to its neighbours. There is no threat from God against those who omit these ascetic practices, but those who are angry without a cause are threatened with hell and hell fire" (83; III.13).

The pastor must be armed against the secret weaknesses of spirit through a constant attention to these concerns. Success takes a combination of piety and considerable intelligence (89; III.15)—where piety includes the kind of self-knowledge and awareness that are the fruit of moral discipline and maturity. In sum:

> Consider, then, what qualities a man needs if he is to withstand such a tempest and deal successfully with these obstacles to the common good. He must be dignified yet modest, impressive yet kindly, masterful yet approachable, impartial yet courteous, humble but not servile, vehement yet gentle, in order that he may be able calmly to resist all these dangers. (93; III.16)

Does Chrysostom demand more than is humanly reasonable or possible? At times throughout the treatise he is certainly prone to hyperbole, as when he exalts the priest into the realm of angels. On occasion his rhetorical temperament seems to push too far in order to make a valid point. Recognize, too, that Chrysostom was also by temperament, as well as conviction, a moralist. This quality is godly when employed with sensitivity and discernment. Restraint in making a case for pastoral purity, however, may be no virtue. Lowered standards (intellectual, moral, or spiritual) neither honor God nor benefit the ministry of the church. Chrysostom sets a very demanding course, but one that he over and over again applied to himself. In fact, one principal reason that he tried to resist ordination is that he believed he could not match up to these standards.

Chrysostom's moral piety also raises important issues for theological education today. Seminaries abound in all manner of excellent courses, including courses on spiritual formation. What often is lacking, however, are courses in moral formation, the very thing that is so prominent among Chrysostom's concerns. As he noted often, morality in one's behavior is something to be learned and which one must work hard to maintain.

Chrysostom's searching analysis of pastoral ministry reveals a depth of theological, psychological, and moral insight. He holds to the highest standards and will tolerate no lessening of these standards, for, he believes, without high standards pastors will be destroyed by the work of ministry and will bring their congregations down with them.

3

Gregory the Great, *Pastoral Care*

No one ventures to teach any art unless he has learned it after deep thought. With what rashness, then, would the pastoral office be undertaken by the unfit, seeing that the government of souls is the art of arts. . . . For no one does more harm in the Church than he, who having the title or rank of holiness, acts evilly.

*(I.2)**

A kindly forewarning is given to pastors lest, while they satisfy the needs of those under them, they slay themselves with the dagger of ambition, and when the neighbours are refreshed with succour given to the body, the pastors themselves remain bereft of the bread of righteousness.

(II.7)

The patristic contribution to the classical tradition in pastoral theology came to its crowning achievement with the publication of Pope Gregory the Great's *Pastoral Care.* Here, Gregory completed the process begun with Gregory of Nazianzus, whom Gregory the Great cites, by writing a book that is simple, subtle, and immediately accessible to any literate clergyman in the ensuing Middle Ages. Of John Chrysostom's *Six Books on the Priesthood* Pope Gregory the Great appears to have no knowledge, most likely because he did not read Greek.

* Gregory the Great: *Regula Pastoralis*, trans. and annotated by Henry Davis, S.J. (New York: Newman Press, 1978), vol. 11, *Ancient Christian Writers: The Works of the Fathers in Translation*, ed. by Johannes Quasten and Joseph C. Plumpe.

Gregory's *Pastoral Care* is the most influential book in the history of the pastoral tradition.[1] It became the dominant treatise on pastoral work for one thousand years—almost immediately after its publication (soon after Gregory became pope) in 590 until the Reformation of the sixteenth century. In the history of the church Gregory's is the most widely read book, after the Bible, on pastoral care.

These bare facts, and the current availability of Gregory's *Pastoral Care* in English, suggest it has continuing significance for the ministry of the church. This historical text has become a classic—that is, a text that is judged to be relevant and valid for every age. It profoundly shaped pastoral care in the medieval age[2]—indeed, Gregory is often regarded in general as the father of the Middle Ages—while its capacity to mould pastoral spirituality and pastoral care today can be confidently predicted if pastors read it. Gregory's *Pastoral Care* is pastoral wisdom literature in the classical tradition in pastoral theology.

GREGORY THE GREAT:
A BRIEF BIOGRAPHY

Gregory lived during a chaotic period and a great turning point of European history. He was born in Rome around 540,[3] son of Gordianus, a wealthy senator, and his wife Silvia. This was no longer imperial Rome, however (the last Roman emperor had fallen in 476), but a city much depleted and bereft of its military and economic might. His family owned large estates in Sicily and a notable mansion in Rome. Gregory's was a pious Christian family; both his mother and two of his father's sisters have been canonized, and Pope Felix (483–492), also canonized, was his ancestor,[4] which no doubt contributed in a powerful way to his early Christian formation.

Little personal information is known about Gregory's early years, but the times were marked by consistent social, military, and economic instability. Between 546 and 552 Rome was successively overrun by invading armies. The second half of the sixth century was also a time of serious economic recession.[5] What effect this military, social, and economic collapse had on the youth we can only imagine. Certainly the mature man believed he was living in the days immediately prior to the end of the world.

We know nothing of his education other than that he probably pursued legal studies as a son of senatorial rank who was preparing for government service. In 573 he was appointed prefect of Rome, the highest legal official in the city. One year later he abandoned civic life, sold his estates, and with the money founded six monasteries. He also turned his Roman home into the Monastery of St. Andrew, and placed himself under the authority of an abbot. "He who had been wont to go about the city clad in the *trabea* and aglow with silk and jewels, now clad in a worthless garment served the altar of the Lord."[6] Gregory referred to the next three years as the happiest of his life. His ascetic lifestyle, however, appears to have had deleterious effects upon his subsequent health.

In 578, as the Lombard armies advanced on Rome, Gregory was ordained a deacon against his will and assumed responsibility for public welfare. Rome was unable to defend herself. Safety seemed to lie with Tiberius, the emperor of the East, and Pope Pelagius II sent Gregory to Constantinople to seek that aid. He was named as a special permanent ambassador to the Eastern court, an appointment that lasted about six years. Gregory failed to obtain the desired military assistance. His years at the Byzantine court were unhappy, mitigated only by the company of fellow monks from the Monastery of St. Andrew who accompanied him and enabled him to continue his monastic discipline. While ambassador, he completed his first major work, *Moralia*, a discussion of moral maxims derived from a metaphorical interpretation of Job.

Recalled to Rome in 586, Gregory soon became abbot of his home monastery. Under his rule the Monastery of St. Andrew prospered, for Gregory was a man of good order and firm leadership. During this time, too, the famous incident occurred when Gregory came across English youths in the Forum—"with fair complexions, handsome faces, and lovely hair," according to the ecclesiastical history of England written by the Venerable Bede.[7] Bede's history, while reading rather hagiographically, provides the reason for Gregory's missionary zeal for the conversion of the Angles, the fair-haired people of the British Isles. He obtained permission from Pope Pelagius II to go in person to Britain with fellow monks as missionaries. Three days after their departure, the people of Rome demanded the return of the beloved abbot, and messengers were dispatched to bring him back, by force if necessary! At a later time, soon after he became pope, Gregory sent missionaries, including Augustine (of Canterbury), to go in his stead, for which initiative the Venerable Bede calls him "our (i.e., England's) apostle."[8]

In 589 Italy suffered an unprecedented flood as the Tiber overflowed its banks, sweeping aside houses, churches, and businesses. The city's corn supplies stored in the bulging granaries of the churches were washed away in the raging waters. Pestilence followed the floods, and the streets of Rome were lined with the rotting bodies of people killed by the plague and the wagons that carried off the bodies to the common graves outside the city walls. In February 590 the pope died of the plague. The church was without a head, and Rome without a guardian and protector.

Almost immediately Gregory was elected pope, much against his will. He wrote to the emperor begging him not to confirm the election, but assumed the role as the plague continued unabated. Always in ill health, and now weak and frail, he nonetheless led the pastoral and relief work with great commitment. Legend has it that because of his petitions, and his leadership of Roman citizens in procession and the prayer, "Lord, have mercy," the Archangel St. Michael was seen atop the mausoleum of Hadrian sheathing his sword as a sign that the plague was now over. Gregory understood this experience in terms of his conviction of a continuing communication between the visible and invisible worlds, a characteristic of Gregory's theology, as we shall see shortly.

Six months after Gregory's election as pope, the emperor confirmed it, Gregory's plans notwithstanding. He tried to flee, but was seized and carried to the Basilica of St. Peter, and on September 3, 590, he was ordained priest and consecrated pope. He was a sick man, wan and frail, and hardly able physically to assume the enormous responsibility placed upon him. The Lombards continued to threaten Rome, the effects of the plague continued to need attention, while various heresies threatened orthodoxy in many parts of the empire. He asked in a sermon soon after his consecration,

> Where, I pray you, is any delight to be found in this world? Mourning meets us everywhere; groans surround us. Ruined cities, fortresses overthrown, lands laid waste, the earth reduced to a desert. . . . There is scarcely a dweller in the cities. The scourge of Heaven's justice strikes without end. . . . What pleasure, then, does life retain, my brethren?[9]

For the remaining fourteen years of his life he regretted his elevation to the papacy. "I undertook the burdens of office with a sick heart," he wrote.[10] Surely he found solace in continuing to wear his monastic habit and in organizing the papal household along monastic principles as he grieved the loss of his peace of soul.

Intestinal disease, gout, and constant fever aside, Gregory worked tirelessly as pope. Almost immediately upon his consecration he published his *Liber pastoralis curae*, *The Book of Pastoral Rule* (published in English as *Pastoral Care*). This book offers the key to his papacy, for Gregory was consistent in that he lived what he preached and ministered what he taught. His piety and humility notwithstanding, and although he called himself "the servant of the servants of God" (*servus servorum domini*), he exercised his office with authority, the first pope to speak *ex cathedra*; he also insisted on the primacy of the see of St. Peter, and especially his primacy over the Eastern Patriarchs. He was only a minor liturgical innovator, though the Gregorian chant is named in honor of him. Amid the destitution of his time, he was generous with the funds of the church, organizing relief work among the poor, starving, and indigent people who had overwhelmed Rome in their search for provision and security. Even as pope, he was the monk who had a care for the world. The threat of attack was never far away, and in 592 hostilities began with the Lombards, who in the following year briefly besieged Rome. Rome had a weak civil administration, and Gregory took matters into his own hands, negotiating a peace with the invaders, while advising generals and providing funds for war munitions. Gregory was *de facto* acting as the civil authority. In the midst of this work, Gregory organized and encouraged the mission to the English, along with parallel missions to Gaul and Africa.

Severe ill health marked the final years of his life. From 598 until his death in March 604, he was largely confined to bed, arising only to celebrate Mass. He was despondent, anticipating the end times, while being as active as he could to bring order to a chaotic world. His epitaph contains the famous notion of Gregory now siting in the council of God:

> Take thy reward in triumph and in joy,
> Who in God's council sit'st eternally.[11]

THEMES IN GREGORY'S THEOLOGY

Although Gregory is one of the four Latin Doctors of the ancient church, along with Ambrose, Jerome, and Augustine of Hippo, he was not a theological innovator,[12] and he accepted the conciliar settlements of the major doctrinal controversies of the prior three hundred years. In fact he was more of a trained administrator than a trained theologian, a man who became a monk by vocation, but was at heart a pastor. Gregory was a child of both Greek tradition and Augustine, synthesizing them, to some extent, with the spirit of desert asceticism. His struggle was practical, not speculative or theoretical. He was Augustinian by conviction, although his worldview differs from the father from Hippo. His achievement was to create the theological synthesis that prepared the way for medieval Christianity. Like Augustine, he had a deep sense of sin and of the incapacity of the will to do good, and always he retained a deep suspicion of those in power—secular or sacred. We will look briefly at three ways that

Gregory's theology had a bearing on pastoral work: (1) the relations between the natural and supernatural worlds, (2) his understanding of *consideratio* and the need for balance between spirituality and action, and (3) the nature of the Christian life.

The Relation between the Natural and Supernatural Worlds

Gregory lived in a sacramental universe, a universe filled with the supernatural breaking through into the natural. In his view, the human stands between the spiritual and the carnal worlds, each person a microcosm of the cosmos, open to favoring one side or the other. Gregory's cosmos, in this regard, was different from that portrayed by Augustine, who was reluctant to speak of interface between the two worlds. With Gregory the boundaries almost vanished. According to American historian Carole Straw, "the supernatural is mingled with the world of ordinary experience, and in surprising ways. Visible and invisible, natural and supernatural, human and divine, carnal and spiritual are often directly and causally connected. Where Augustine stresses the mystery and ambiguity of signs, hiding yet hinting at supernatural realities, Gregory is far more interested in carnal signs as mediating links between this world and the spiritual reality beyond."[13] Just as Gregory saw the Bible as having a spiritual and a literal or historical dimension, so he saw a world with a supernatural and a natural level, the former operating just outside sense perception, yet knowable insofar as it breaks through from time to time.[14]

The danger here, of course, is the tendency to overly spiritualize the world. Gregory had a sense of the credibility of the incredible, an uncritical credulity, perhaps, in which he could believe all kinds of tales about relics, for example. Yet for Gregory God was understood to more closely order events in the world. God, in Gregory's view, is intimately connected with physical experience. Even suffering in such a view is directly attributable to God. The corollary to this is that the experiences of our lives in the world can mediate things of God. Thus while Gregory's understanding is of a God who is remote and to be feared, nevertheless the universe is imbued with Divinity, and therefore, for all of his spiritual demeanor, Gregory remains committed to the world, believing that experience, both spiritual and carnal, is an organic whole.[15]

It was in line with this belief system that Gregory fought on two fronts on behalf of his people, both to care for their bodies amid famine, plague, war and economic disaster and to guide them away from attraction to spiritual entities not blessed by God, to return to the worship and service of the true God.

Consideratio

A key concept of Gregorian spirituality is the notion of *consideratio*, which means the exercise of introspection that examines both inner motives and experiences and outer actions in such a way that a balance is established between them.[16] *Consideratio* is concerned to achieve a right relationship between body and soul by applying reflection and reason. This intentionality led to Gregory's sense of harmony between contemplation and action—still a remarkably fresh and provocative synthesis.

Gregory worked toward achieving a balance in the ordering of the two worlds, the spiritual and the carnal, in a way that reflected his understanding of God's paradoxical ordering of the universe. Reconciliation and complementarity[17] marked his understanding of a sacramental universe. He advocated a moderate, reflective middle course that led to a life of humility and hope, contemplation and activity. Good, he believed, is found in balance; activity precedes contemplation, and contemplation must be expressed in service. Gregory found this model in Christ, and thought it applied to more than just religious life. Gregory was concerned also to order secular life in such a way that it, too, be kept in balance.

Consideratio is a monastic virtue taught in the Rule of St. Benedict, but it is not to be confused with *contemplatio*. Contemplation means loving God with single-minded devotion. In the midst of an active life that involves feeding, teaching, caring, and so on, *consideratio* required the balancing of spiritual and physical, personal and social dimensions of experience. It allows one to look heavenward and earthward as a practical discipline. *Consideratio* was a mental discipline wherein the things of this world are put into the perspective of the spiritual world. The results are that one understands the active life from a spiritual frame of reference and lives it, therefore, in a reflective, balanced way.

Especially for this pope, this balance was difficult but necessary to maintain. Gregory often complained that he found it hard, and even impossible: "Often it happens that when a man undertakes the cares of government, his heart is distracted with a diversity of things, and as his mind is divided among many interests and becomes confused, he finds he is unfitted for any of them" (I.4, 27[18]). The problem in this case is a lack of *consideratio*. The discussion in Book II of Gregory's *Pastoral Care* is an illustration of balanced *consideratio* that is no doubt what he worked hard to achieve: be discretely silent, yet speak appropriately (II.4, 51); be a neighbor in compassion, yet aloof in thought (II.5, 56); be humble in company with those who live good lives, yet stand up against evil doers with zeal for righteousness (II.6, 59); and be balanced in care between one's inner and outer life (II.7, 68). We must always be vigilant, he wrote to the Abbot of Lerins, maintaining the tension so as to maintain balance.[19]

The Nature of the Christian life

Gregory was a pastor, and he knew that human life is fragile. He understood the meaning of the Fall and the role that sin plays in our lives. If balance in all things is desirable, its opposite is a chaotic and bewildering inconstancy in which we are ever more deeply confused. "If we consider the journey of this life truthfully, we find nothing firm nor stable in it,"[20] he noted. The "sorrows of mutability" characterize human existence since Adam rejected stability in relationship with God. Gregory wrote of a "slippery mutability" that leads to disharmony, strife, and insecurity.[21] Thus, like Augustine, Gregory saw humankind in a perilous state in which we can do nothing of our own free will to help ourselves. Unlike Augustine, however, he saw sin arising from the conflict between the soul and the body rather than from the will. Our desire is for pleasure, he believed, and this drives us towards the world and away from God. The Fall has meant that we are now the devil's purchase. Our discipline and self-control, as well as our minds, are corrupted. We cannot be still enough even to know God and know the right.

Gregory believed in prevenient grace, a grace that is prior to everything else, that comes first of all. But this grace enables and demands good works, for in salvation the human also must act. For Gregory, just as Christ comes as a savior with gentleness, he comes also demanding a way of life; for those who are disobedient, he comes again with judgment. God's mercy means that God accepts what we offer, and our task is to offer what will be acceptable. Ambivalence and terror, for Gregory, never go away. Always fear remains, for we can never know the extent of God's judgment. Gregory thus understood the Christian life as one of sacrifice and suffering. As such, life's moral purpose is to serve others. A good person is not corrupted by the world but may find some confidence in the very redemption sought through good works, and although never free from temptation or persecution, a person may nonetheless have a stillness and calm amid the torrents. Always, in Gregory's view, we remain poised between salvation and judgment, trusting in God's mercy, yet never relaxing our vigilance.[22]

In the frame of reference bounded by these theological ideas, Gregory sets the work of the rector. The pastor's work bears upon eternity, both for the pastor and the members of the congregation.

PASTORAL CARE

Gregory's *Pastoral Care* carries the Latin title, *Liber regulae pastoralis: The Book of Pastoral Rule*. The title immediately betrays its author's monastic influence, for the book is intended to be a rule for pastors (and bishops) modeled on a monastic rule, to guide life and work. In fact, the book provided the secular clergy's counterpart to a monastic rule, and it was received with enthusiasm and read widely. Gregory's *Pastoral Care* was immediately translated into Greek at the command of the Emperor Maurice. First translated into West Saxon English in the ninth century, the work was already known in the English church, for Alcuin wrote to the Bishop of York in 796, "Wherever you go, let the pastoral book of St. Gregory be your companion. Read and re-read it often, that in it you may know yourself and your work, that you may have before your eyes how you ought to live and teach. The book is a mirror of the life of a bishop and a medicine for all the wounds inflicted by the Devil's deception."[23] In Europe, Charlemagne in 813 had made the study of Gregory's *Pastoral Care* obligatory of all his bishops. Later bishops at their consecration customarily received a copy of Gregory's books along with a copy of the canons of the church, with the admonition to observe its teaching in their pastoral work.[24]

Writing of Gregory over a century ago, one historian opined that "many of the Fathers of the Church have surpassed him in style and eloquence; his style is too redundant, too evidently marked by the rhetorical habits of a declining age; but no man ever understood the human soul better, analysed more closely its miseries and necessities, or indicated with greater clearness and energy the remedy for these evils."[25] With these words in mind we will cover three topics discussed by Gregory: (1) what manner of person should take on the office of pastoral charge over people, (2) the life of the pastor, and (3) the practice and complexities of pastoral work.

The Faithful Pastor

In the first part of his *Pastoral Care*, Gregory investigates in a general way the character of the person who would be a pastor. The first lesson is that a pastor must be taught the art of pastoral work. Gregory is aware that pastoral ignorance has the effect of leaving the people with the burden of their sins (I.1, 23). Thus,

> No one ventures to teach any art unless he has learned it after deep thought. With what rashness, then, would the government of souls be

> undertaken by the unfit, seeing that the government of souls is the art
> of arts! (I.1, 21)

Gregory sums up his argument in two syllogisms.[26] First: Every art must be learned; the government of souls is the art of arts; thus, the government of souls must be learned. Second: Dangerous diseases must be treated by qualified physicians; diseases of the soul are the most dangerous of all diseases; thus, sin-sickness must be treated by qualified physicians of the soul. Pastors, in other words, must be especially fit through education and maturity for office.

Sadly, however, he reflects, people who are untrained as physicians of the soul are not afraid to aspire to pastoral office. They are driven by vanity and remain unfit to be pastors, aspiring to the *magisterium humilitatis* for the sake of the honor it confers. They long to rule over others, hear their praises sung, enjoy the position of honor, and rejoice in the affluence of gain (I.8, 35). Their imaginations are filled with thoughts of doing good things, but one filled with potential for self-deception.

> When the mind has begun to enjoy, in a worldly fashion, the office of
> superiority which it has got, it readily forgets all the spiritual thoughts
> it had . . . for a man is quite incapable of learning humility in a posi-
> tion of superiority . . . Therefore, let everyone discover from his past
> life what manner of man he is, lest the phantasy of his thoughts deceive
> him when he craves for superiority. (I.9, 36–7)

Gregory warns would-be pastors that

> a man who is weak yearns after the burden of office, and one who is
> extremely likely to fall under his own burden is willing to be over-
> whelmed by putting his shoulders beneath the burdens of others! He
> cannot bear his own deeds, and increases the burden he bears! (I.7, 34)

Gregory broadens the concern for fitness to include what today we would call congruence and integrity. Those persons should not be pastors, he argues, who do not live what they profess. "There are some who investigate spiritual precepts with shrewd diligence, but in the life they live trample on what they have penetrated by their understanding" (I.2, 23). A most interesting exercise would be to put the issue of fitness for office on Gregory's terms to denominational and seminary leaders responsible for the education and selection of persons for ministry. Applying Gregory's standards to theological education today, one is not yet fit to be a pastor just because he or she has passed the theology test and completed a course or two in pastoral care (and who has a Master of Divinity degree and field education experience), if his or her conduct and life are not congruent with this learning. Such unfit pastors are a menace to ministry, and serve only to hurt the people they ostensibly want to serve. Mixing his metaphors, but making his point nevertheless, Gregory notes that the sheep, sadly, drink of the water befouled by the feet of these unworthy pastors when they follow their example (I,2, 24). Gregory puts his salutary warning as bluntly as possible:

> No one does more harm in the Church than he, who having the title or rank of holiness, acts evilly. . . . If a man vested with the appearance of holiness destroys others by word or example, it certainly were better for him that his earthly deeds, performed in a worldly guise, should press him to death, rather than that his sacred offices should have pointed him out to others for sinful imitation; surely the punishment of Hell would prove less severe for him if he fell alone. (I.2, 24)

A sure test of unfitness for pastoral office is distraction. Gregory makes two points in this regard. First, Gregory mentions the distraction of being well paid. Not many pastors likely have this problem today, yet pastors who are poorly paid may also be greatly distracted by anger on account of their pittance. Neither extreme should determine a pastor's sense of self. Prosperity, argues Gregory, fills us with pride, while adversity is to be disregarded. "Let him not be elated by prosperity, nor disconcerted by adversity" (II.3, 49). Second, distraction can interfere with ministry insofar as our minds can be overwhelmed by the many demands made upon us. The result: "it is as though (the mind) were so preoccupied during a journey as to forget what its destination was" (I.4, 27). Gregory's point is that concentration on external things leads to a loss of inward or interior awareness, and positively, that balance must prevail in all things. This is the application of *consideratio*. A loss of focus and a lack of balance are very dangerous: "we would not have men who stumble on plain ground, to set their feet on a precipice" (I.4, 29). Much better for all of them and the people who would be under their pastoral leadership for the former to seek an alternative occupation, leaving the care of souls to more competent men and women.

After these warnings, Gregory goes on to say that people who are called to ministry and are qualified must not resist the call. A love of quiet and a desire for peace must not be selfishly pursued at the expense of serving people to whom one is called to minister. People who are called and are qualified have gifts that should be used for the sake of the church. For the want of using them, the pastor also in the end deprives himself or herself of the very peace that he or she wanted to protect. Such unfaithful pastors "are certainly guilty in proportion to the public service which they were able to afford" (I.5, 31). To make his point, Gregory develops an odd analogy from Deuteronomy 25:5–10, regarding levirate marriage. God's law demanded that the brother of a dead man should marry his late brother's widow. If he did not, she was to spit in his face, and her relatives were to take one shoe from his feet and call his home the house of the unshod. According to Gregory's allegorical interpretation, the dead brother is the risen Lord, who said, "Go and tell my brothers" (Matt. 28:10), for all of the elect have not yet heard the gospel. The surviving "brother"—the disciple, in other words—is to take the "wife"—that is, the church—and care for her. To whoever does not, the church spits in his face, and a shoe is taken from his feet. "If therefore," concludes Gregory, "we have the care of our neighbors as well as of ourselves, we protect each foot with a shoe. But a man who, thinking only of his own advantage, disregards that of his neighbors, loses with disgrace the shoe, as it were, of one foot" (I.5, 31). In other words, if you are not faithful to your call, you will hop along like a one-shoed person!

Gregory argues that to reject a call to ministry when one is well qualified and graced for the work is false humility. Thus the general axiom: "One who has not been cleansed, must not dare to undertake sacred ministries; and one who has been cleansed by supernal graces, must not proudly resist under the guise of humility" (I.7, 33). Typical of Gregorian antinomies, a false humility may hide a corresponding pride!

Gregory's advice, then, is that a person suited for pastoral office must affirm the call to ministry, but know what is involved. Such a person must make an inventory of the necessary virtues to do the job and be plainly aware of what is involved, both in terms of the skills required and the kind of life appropriate to the calling (I.8, 35). Today we would speak of self-knowledge, for the lack of which pride rushes in. Later when we consider the teaching of Richard Baxter, the English Puritan, we will see that Baxter's first principle is an echo of Gregory's teaching: "Take heed to yourself" (Acts 20:28), and that Baxter spends considerable space in *The Reformed Pastor* exploring this theme. Thus we find a basic truth for anyone considering ministry, a truth spread across the centuries of the church and attested by the greatest pastors who have served in her ministry: attend to your own spiritual, moral, and theological maturity.

Finally, Gregory turns directly to the character of the pastor. Following the teaching of the emerging classical tradition in pastoral theology (of which he is a part) that demands the highest standards, Gregory counsels that a pastor must

> devote himself entirely to setting an ideal of living. He must die to all
> passions of the flesh and by now lead a spiritual life. He must have put
> aside worldly prosperity; he must fear no adversity, desire only what is
> interior. He must be a man whose aims are not thwarted by a body out
> of perfect accord through frailty, nor by contumacy of the spirit. He
> is not led to covet the goods of others, but is bounteous in giving of
> his own. He is quickly moved by a compassionate heart to forgive. . . .
> [H]e sympathizes with the frailties of others, and so rejoices in the
> good. . . . He so studies to live as to be able to water the dry hearts of
> others. . . . By his practice and experience of prayer he has learned
> already that he can obtain from the Lord what he asks for. (I.10, 38)

Oden calls this "situational discernment" and "wisdom,"[27] and he is correct, yet it is also a quality of life and a maturity of spirit that must mark out the character and actions of a pastor.

Gregory concludes Book I and his discussion of the character of the pastor with a remarkable allegorical reading of a curious passage, Leviticus 21:17–20, which is concerned with the deformities and infirmities that exclude a man from the Aaronic priesthood. The various prohibitions become symbols in Gregory's mind for character defects that should exclude a person from ministry. In summary fashion, Gregory ends by stating that

> whosoever, then, is subject to any of the aforesaid defects, is forbidden
> to offer loaves of bread to the Lord. The reason is obvious: a man
> who is still ravaged by his own sins, cannot expiate the sins of others."
> (I.11, 44)

In spite of a writing style that is rather flowery and at times overly allegorical by modern tastes and standards, Gregory manages to deliver a simple but provocative dual message in these opening chapters: The person who would be a pastor has theological, professional, moral, and spiritual maturity, and exercises personal accountability for this maturity through rigorous self-examination of conscience. Because he is aware of our capacity for deceit and lack of awareness regarding our own sin, Gregory demands rigorous honesty. Everyone who would be faithful in the work of pastoral care is faced with a concern for the state of his or her own soul and the quality of his or her own life before God. This theme is found in every text in our study and is a major characteristic of the classical tradition in pastoral theology. If the authors lean heavily toward scrupulousness and insist on a standard that may demand more than most pastors today feel they can meet, the goal nevertheless in each case is the encouragement of spiritual and moral maturity and theological competence, necessities for a ministry that is serious about its godly work. Not an acceptable mediocrity but the very best fitness for ministry is to be expected.

Neither is Gregory's concern for the very highest standards a prosaic point for mainline churches today, given the concerns for and confusions about ministry that abound everywhere. A reading of Gregory's *Pastoral Care* raises an institutional question for consideration: Are the men and women emerging from our theological academies and candidacy processes competently prepared for office? While we do well with skills training compared with times past, the theological, moral, and spiritual education and formation of pastors are the subjects of continuing debate amid the sense that we are in a difficult time for ministers. Conflict between congregations and their clergy is rising. Both the lower number of persons entering ministry, and the sense that they are less qualified academically and spiritually, and with a more limited personal history in the church, have become matters of ongoing concern. Further, ministers are leaving the profession at such a rate that, with declining recruitment, many mainline denominations now face a serious clergy shortage for the immediate future. These conditions indicate that all is not well with ministry. In such a context it is interesting that the Association of Theological Schools in the United States and Canada is pressing seminaries and divinity schools to focus especially on the question of whether or not their graduates are well prepared for the practice of ministry. The question is, are the institutions that prepare men and women for ministry doing a good job? Gregory's concern for theological, moral, and spiritual competency for ministry is again before the mind of the church.

The Life of the Pastor

In Part II of the book Gregory develops further and in a practical way some themes found already in Part I. He begins, however, with a theme from Gregory of Nazianzus, namely, that the conduct of a pastor should be far superior to the conduct of others. Then he identifies eight characteristics essential for the lives of the clergy. A pastor

> must carefully consider how necessary it is for him to maintain a life of rectitude. It is necessary, therefore, that he should be pure in thought, exemplary in conduct, discreet in keeping silence, profitable in speech, in sympathy a near neighbour to everyone, in contemplation exalted above all others, a humble companion to those who lead good lives, erect in his zeal for righteousness against the vices of sinners.

Gregory then adds a summary that is an example of the simplicity of *consideratio*, yet which heightens our sense of its complexity in practice:

> He must not be remiss in his care for the inner life by preoccupation with the external; nor must he in his solicitude for what is internal, fail to give attention to the external. (II.1, 45)

Next Gregory discusses each of these themes, each case being an illustration of the pastoral balance that is such a marked feature of Gregorian pastoral care. What follows is Gregory's list of characteristics necessary for a faithful pastor.

The pastor must ever be pure in thought. Gregory states that "it is necessary that the hand that aims at cleansing filth should itself be clean, lest, sordid with clinging dirt, it fouls for the worse everything it touches" (II.2, 46). Three areas of expertise are involved in practice: use of right reason, continuing reflection on the tradition of the church (walking in "the footsteps of the saints" [II.2, 47]), and the discernment of good from evil. In this way the pastor exercises good judgment through sound doctrine and careful discernment of the truth, and operates with the mind of Christ, rooting out all self-interest.

The pastor must be exemplary in conduct. The manner of a pastor's life must show the way of God to the flock, who follow both by teaching and example. Thus, the pastor's "voice penetrates the hearts of his hearers the more readily, if his way of life commends what he says" (II.3, 48). Gregory later elaborates on this point: "Doctrine taught does not penetrate the minds of the needy, if a compassionate heart does not commend it to the hearts of hearers; but the seed of the word does germinate promptly, when the kindness of a preacher waters it in the hearer's heart" (II.7, 72). By a pastor's manner of life his or her voice is able to speak from the heights and be heard. A pastor is thus separated out from everyone else insofar as his or her life surpasses even the well-doer in goodness. "Let him not be elated by prosperity, nor disconcerted by adversity. Let not the smooth enervate his will, nor the rough cast him down to despair" (II.3, 49).

The pastor should be discreet in keeping silence and profitable in speech. Knowing when to speak and when to keep silent is a vital pastoral insight. The pastor must be able to speak boldly and candidly in the face of danger to the people of God or when sin must be named. Further, like a bell sounding clear and distinct, the pastor is a herald who must announce the way of the Lord. But when speech is hastily spoken or ill-ordered, the hearts of the people may be stricken with the wound of error (II.4, 54). Pastors must be careful to see to it "that not only should nothing evil proceed from their lips, but that not even what is proper be said in excess or in a slovenly manner" (II.4, 54). The issue, again, is one of balance.

The pastor should be a neighbor in compassion to all and exalted above all in thought. Thus by the love of his or her heart the pastor must draw near to all who hurt, yet by contemplation transcend his or her own woundedness that accrues from solidarity with the pain of others, and thus maintain a right relationship with God. Too much compassion and the pastor ceases to seek that which is above; too much contemplation and the pastor neglects his or her neighbors. Gregory understands the biblical nature of compassion as a taking into oneself the suffering of others, and he knows well its dangers.[28] Again, the lesson is one of balance:

> [T]rue preachers do not only aspire by contemplation to the Holy Head of the Church above, namely, the Lord, but also descend to its members in pity for them. . . . Inwardly he considers the hidden things of God, outwardly he bears the burdens of carnal men." (II.6, 57)

This, says Gregory, is the model of Jesus Christ: a balance between prayer and ministry. By this rhythm of ministry pastors show their parishioners a gentle, approachable face so that "they will have recourse to the pastor's understanding as to a mother's bosom" (II.6, 58).

Servanthood and authority should characterize the pastoral office. Gregory's discussion of this theme (Book II, Chapter 6) marks the heart of Gregory's teaching by way of a careful exposition of balance in the development of his central metaphor for ministry. This is the center of Gregory's pastoral theology:

> [A]ll who are superiors (bishops and pastors) should not regard in themselves the power of their rank, but the equality of their nature; and they should find their joy not in ruling over men, but in helping them. . . . (They are to be) not kings of men, but shepherds of flocks." (II.6, 60)

The pastor as a shepherd of the people is Gregory's central metaphor for pastoral work. Now there are times when the pastor must "lord it over" others, for instance when confronting people who lead evil lives. "Supreme rank is, therefore, well-administered, when the superior lords it over vices rather than over brethren" (II.6, 63–64). False humility is dangerous in the care of souls if a pastor is unwilling to chastise sinners appropriately (II.6, 65). But generally speaking, Gregory is nervous about the personal assumption of power, which leads to conceit, bloated self-aggrandizement, and pride. The issue, then, is due proportionality, to know how to assert power when necessary and when to oppose it (II.6, 62).

Tension exists between authority and humility in the exercise of pastoral care. Discipline must be exercised rightly by a humble pastor, thus the maxim: "the greater the external manifestation of power, the more is it to be kept in subjection internally" (II.6, 65). Gregory warns, too, that the pastor who diverts the ministry of pastoral care to purposes of domination is a hypocrite. Even a hard word spoken in pastoral care must be moderated with kindness, like that of a mother, lest discipline be too harsh or rigid. In fact, says Gregory, discipline and compassion should be exercised dependently on one another. Pastors "in their relations with subjects should be animated by compassion duly considerate and by discipline affectionately severe" (II.6, 66)—a balanced use of oil and vinegar, balm and purgative, the rod and manna.

The pastor should stay mindful of the balance between spirituality and ministry. Gregory now returns to a theme that is becoming familiar to his readers.

> Let the ruler not relax the care of the inner life by preoccupying himself with external matters, nor should his solicitude for the inner life bring neglect of the external, lest, being engrossed with what is external, he be ruined inwardly, or being preoccupied with what concerns only his inner self, he does not bestow on his neighbours the necessary external care. (II.7, 68)

Gregory's comments have contemporary application for he names specifically the pastor who, in today's language, is compulsively and codependently driven to overwork:

> They take it as a pleasure to be weighed down by such activities. . . . They disregard those interior matters which they ought to be teaching others. (II.7, 68)

> Woe betides the congregation eagerly following a pastor who has lost his or her way: When earthly cares occupy the pastor's mind, dust, driven by the winds of temptation, blinds the eyes of the Church. (II.7, 69)

Pastors must be on guard against busyness, being careless in attention to their spiritual and moral lives. Here

> a kindly forewarning is given to pastors lest, while they satisfy the needs of those under them, they slay themselves with the dagger of ambition, and when the neighbours are refreshed with succour given to the body, the pastors themselves remain bereft of the bread of righteousness. (II.7, 73)

Without the pastors' spiritual self-care, congregations are led by blind guides who destroy themselves and their congregations.

On the other hand (of course!), Gregory warns also against pastors being so preoccupied with their spiritual state that they neglect the care of their bodies. Citing Ezekiel 44:20, Gregory warns that pastors "are rightly forbidden to shave the head, or let the hair grow long, that so they may not wholly disregard all considerations of the flesh" (II.7, 74).

Pastors must balance pleasing people and speaking the truth. Gregory counsels pastors against so desiring to please people that they fail to speak the truth to them: "For that man is an enemy of his Redeemer who on the strength of the good works he performs, desires to be loved by the Church, rather than by Him" (II.8, 75). Such desire for external praise compromises ministry: "To put cushions under every elbow is to cherish with smooth flattery souls that are fallen away from rectitude in the pleasures of this world" (II.8, 75). Pastors find it easy to flatter people who intimidate them, while treating harshly those who, in their estimation, can do nothing against them. "He, therefore, who sets himself to act evilly and yet wishes others to be silent, is a witness against himself, for he wishes to be loved more than the truth" (II.8, 76).

But consider another side also, for there is a right sense in which pastors need to be loved, namely, in order that people will listen to them and the pastor will be in a position to bring others to Christ:

> Good rulers should wish to please men, but so as to draw their neighbors to the love of truth by the fair esteem they have of their rulers. . . .
> It is difficult for one who is not loved, however well he preaches, to find a sympathetic hearing. Wherefore, he who rules ought to aim at being loved, that he may be listened to, and yet not seek to be loved on his own account, lest he be discovered to rebel in the tyranny of his thought against Him whom he ostensibly serves in his office. (II.8, 77)

Again we see Gregory's remarkable sense of balance and knowledge of pastoral work.

A pastor must be a person of the Word of God. Whatever else is necessary, a pastor must meditate daily on the precepts of the Bible, for ministry is rooted in scripture. The fact is, says Gregory, converse with the world, the stuff of pastoral work, will destroy "the sense of responsibility and a provident circumspection in regard to the celestial life" (II.11, 87). Thus, people who would be pastors should "never depart from the occupation of sacred reading" (II.11, 88).

Book II, which ends with an anchoring word that in effect sums up everything that Gregory has already written, is largely self-evident and requires little additional commentary or comment. Gregory's spiritual insights into the lives of pastors, coupled with his sense of balance, make his counsels the epitome of practical personal wisdom, for which reason his *Pastoral Care* has stood the test of time.

The Practice and Complexities of Pastoral Work

Again citing Gregory of Nazianzus, Gregory the Great adopts the dictum that the same pastoral practice is not suitably applied to every person. People are highly complex, and to each must be given what is necessary and appropriate. To illustrate the contextual nature of pastoral work (Gregory casts his teaching as advice to preachers, but it applies equally to pastoral work), he develops thirty-six "admonitions" in the style of antinomies—today we would call them case study illustrations of pastoral opposites—in which he spells out the pastoral necessity of responding variously to particular exigencies of parishioners.

> Well, as long before us Gregory of Nazianzus of revered memory has taught, one and the same exhortation is not suited to all, because they are not compassed by the same quality of character. Often, for instance, what is profitable to some, harms others. . . . Wherefore, the discourse of a teacher should be adapted to the character of his hearers, so as to be suited to the individual in his respective needs, and yet never deviate from the art of general edification. (III.Prologue, 89)

Gregory operates with a number of working assumptions in his practice of pastoral care. First, he insists that the pastor should understand that vices commonly masquerade as virtues (II.9, 78). A mean person may pass himself off as frugal, while one who is an inappropriate spendthrift may pass himself or herself off as openhanded. Thus a pastor must be able to discern virtue from vice, and to suspect that a virtue openly displayed may hide a corresponding vice.

Second, Gregory recognizes that prudence is required at all times in giving pastoral counsel. Some obvious faults, for example, should be tolerated when the occasion is not right for reprimand; wounds, Gregory observes, are more inflamed by untimely incisions (II.10, 79). On the other hand, sometimes digging deeply into a person is necessary, when from apparently insignificant appearances something of a more serious nature is suspected.

Third, a pastor must know when to intrude into a person's life with gentleness, as when sin is committed, not through malice, but through sheer ignorance or frailty. Reproof must be tempered with forbearance (II.10, 82). In fact, Gregory suggests that pastors should be on the lookout with respect to their own responses, for whenever a pastor is overly zealous in reproach she or he may be acting in response to fearing in her or his own case that which she or he reproves in another. Thomas C. Oden has helpfully noted that this observation is akin to the psychoanalytic notion of projection,[29] and is to be avoided.

Nevertheless, fourth, some things must be reproved severely, lest a person's sin is not otherwise recognized. Gregory insists that sometimes a pastor must "correct with severe and zealous asperity those evils in his subjects which cannot be treated with forbearance, lest, being too little incensed against such faults, he himself be held guilty of all" (II.10, 83). But even so, Gregory warns against an immoderate counsel, lest the hearts of the sinners fall into dejection and despair.

> The axe flies from the hand when reproof oversteps itself and degenerates into asperity; and the iron flies from the handle, when the words of reproof are excessively harsh and the friend is struck and killed; that is to say, a contumelious utterance kills the spirit of love in the hearer. (II.10, 86)

To illustrate these general points, Gregory sets forth a series of brief discussions or case studies about the manner of care suitable for various types and classes of people. Thus, for example, he discusses the care of men and women, the young and the old, the poor and the rich, the joyful and the sad, slaves and masters, the sincere and the insincere, the well and the sick, the humble and the haughty, those living in discord and those living in peace, and so on.[30] The abiding theme throughout the discussions of the polarities is that above all else God's love must be communicated amid the varied responses.[31] Gregory amply illustrates that he is a student of people and the manifold issues that life produces. In every circumstance he is a skilled physician to their souls, a faithful father in Christ to those given into his charge.

Gregory ends by noting that he has tried to show what a pastor should be like. He acknowledges that he has painted the portrait of an ideal pastor, and that he, Gregory, while directing others to perfection, has far fallen short of the picture he presented (IV.1, 237).

Gregory's *Pastoral Care* is a book of practical pastoral wisdom, challenging psychological honesty and keen spiritual insight. His work does not have the sense of theological or personal anxiety found in Gregory of Nazianzus and John Chrysostom, in large part because Gregory assumed most theological questions were settled, although he lived in a deeply unsettled time. *Pastoral Care* is a book for the church investing in the long haul rather than the church trying to survive a present crisis. For that reason Gregory's work was admirably equipped to guide the church through the Middle Ages and into the Reformation.

Gregory shares with the classical writers before and following him the themes that define the classical tradition, especially the sense of the call to moral, spiritual, and theological maturity; the sense of accountability before God for the faithful exercise of pastoral care; a conviction that pastoral work must deal with people in their lives with God; and an awareness of the complexity of the pastoral task. He is especially distinguished in his attention also to the small and ordinary areas of life's experience. In this sensitivity to and care for personal detail, Gregory shows himself to be truly a pastor of the flock of Christ.

4

Martin Bucer,
On the True Pastoral Care

Bucer . . . "the pastor of nations . . ."

John Milton

The goal and end of this seeking and leading to Christ of lost sheep
. . . is to bring them into the fold of Christ, so that they give themselves wholly to Christ . . . hear his voice in all things, and use all
those things which the Lord has appointed for furthering the salvation of his sheep . . . In a word, in the community of Christ alone
the salvation of Christ is to be received.

Von der waren Seelsorge[1]

Martin Bucer's *On the True Pastoral Care* (*Von der waren Seelsorge*[2]) is the
principal Reformation text on pastoral theology. In it Bucer makes a significant contribution toward developing the theological identity of
pastoral work within Protestantism. Bucer's pastoral theology is important because it is rooted directly in biblical and Reformation faith and
is oriented to the practical care of souls. Bucer is largely unknown as a
pastoral theologian in English-speaking Christianity because his work
lacks an English translation, remaining still only in German, Latin, and
Czech.[3]

Words of praise for Bucer's work as it relates to pastoral care are easily found from historians and theologians. J. T. McNeill regarded
Bucer's work on pastoral care as "the most outstanding" Reformation
text on the subject,[4] and he suggested its lasting value for Protestantism
as being of a similar caliber to Richard Baxter's *The Reformed Pastor*.[5]
According to W. P. Stephens Bucer's book is "almost a running exegesis
of scriptural quotations. What (Bucer) is concerned to do is to discover

the scriptural tests of a ministry that is of the Holy Spirit and not of men."[6] David F. Wright credits it as "surely one of the noblest pastoral treatises to come out of the whole Reformation movement."[7] Thomas F. Torrance describes it as an "all-important little work," not least because in it Bucer's Reformation-shaping patristic study is seen particularly clearly.[8] For Torrance it is an epoch-making text.[9] Finally, and most recently, Amy Nelson Burnett describes it as "his masterwork of pastoral theology."[10] Curiously, in the light of these comments, W. A. Clebsch and C. R. Jaekle omitted any exhibit from Bucer in their *Pastoral Care in Historical Perspective*, a contributing factor in English-speaking pastoral theology being largely unaware of Bucer's work in modern times.[11]

These testimonies indicate that Bucer's pastoral theology is a work pastors can learn from, not only as an exhibit from church history, but more importantly as a text from the Reformation that can speak directly to the practice of pastoral work today. Its value lies in the clear theological framework into which Bucer cast all pastoral work. Torrance believes that "history has not yet taken its full measure of Martin Butzer (Bucer) who must be adjudged as standing within the sphere of Reformed rather than Lutheran theology, not only because of his masterful influence on Calvin or Calvin's considerable influence on him, but because his pioneer work in Biblical hermeneutics and patristic study helped shape the whole Reformed Church."[12] Bucer illustrates the dictum that if one would be a faithful and competent pastor, one had better be a good biblical scholar and theologian! That he remains still a "'reformer in the wings," in spite of being one of the most influential figures on the European continent at the time,[13] should not be taken to infer that his work is not of enduring significance for the church.

MARTIN BUCER: A BRIEF BIOGRAPHY

Bucer was a biblical scholar and theologian of the highest rank, a diplomat, and a churchman of distinction. He founded no denomination, although his influence upon both Luther and Calvin was considerable. He was a spokesman for reform, a vigorous polemicist, an ecclesiastical organizer of consummate talent, an advocate for church unity—especially with regard to the Lord's Supper and the division between Protestants and Roman Catholics—and a liturgical innovator of enduring significance, most notably influencing Thomas Cranmer in the writing of the *Book of*

Common Prayer. He was a friend and mentor to Reformers far and near, well known especially as the teacher of John Calvin during the latter's sojourn in Strasbourg.

Born in November 1491 in Schlettstadt, Alsace, the son of a cobbler, he discovered early a passion for learning. He was a student in the town's Latin school, moving in 1506 to the Dominicans' house as a postulant, where he of course studied Thomas Aquinas. In 1512 he entered the cloister of the Blackfriars in Heidelberg, where he continued his education, becoming acquainted also with the works of the humanist scholar Erasmus and of the young Martin Luther. As a young Dominican theologian he attended a colloquy in April 1518 at which he encountered Luther in person, when the reformer from Wittenberg came to Heidelberg to defend his theses on the misuse of indulgences. Bucer was spellbound, much to the dismay of his superiors. The meeting with Luther was the catalyst that transformed his life. While a student at Heidelberg, Bucer began, as he put it, to "dis-relish Poperie."

Bucer was twenty-nine years of age when, early in 1521, he left the monastery to take up the duties of a parish priest. While still holding this office, the next year he married Elizabeth Silbereisen, a former nun, who was a most faithful companion, tending to his needs in a quiet, unobtrusive way that allowed him much freedom to be about his work without household cares.[14] The next two years were somewhat chaotic, as he searched for his life's way amid the politics, and sometimes the violence, of reform. Association with Luther, marriage, and the public exposition of his own developing views regarding reform of theology and church led to excommunication from the Church of Rome. He did then what countless troubled persons before and since have done when in dire distress: he went home to his parents, fleeing to Strasbourg, now his father's home and a city already in the throes of reform. Strasbourg became the city with which his name is forever linked. From uninvited and barely tolerated resident alien, with time he became the leading pastor and theologian of the town, and from this base—after 1524 when he was installed as pastor of the parish of St. Aurelia—he set forth to make his mark on church and state. Quickly he emerged to participate in and to some extent even to dominate the theological colloquies and the politics of reform in Germanic Europe for a quarter of a century. He remained a pastor in the city until his exile to England twenty-five years later.

Bucer relished center stage and delighted in theological debate and the politics of reform. Yet his engagement was not for the sake of power, but for the sake of the reform and the good order of the church. For example, in 1529, Bucer attempted to mediate between the Swiss and German reformers on the issue of the Lord's Supper by advocating a middle position—a policy of compromise—between Zwingli and Luther, leading finally in 1536 to the Wittenberg Concord. Zwingli and Luther had clashed from 1524 and for five years hence over the meaning of the words, "This is my body." Zwingli held to a symbolic interpretation, while Luther held to a doctrine of the real presence. A colloquy, summoned by Phillip of Hesse, was arranged to settle the issue. Bucer believed the dispute could be settled, and although agreement was not reached in 1529, he traveled Europe in his attempts to heal the rift between the two parties. Finally, however, even after an agreement appeared to have been reached in 1536, the Swiss remained unhappy with the result, and the effort failed. Even more radically perhaps, in 1540 Bucer attempted a mediation between Protestants and irenic Roman Catholics, which came to fruit with the colloquy at Regensburg in 1541, with agreement on the Fall, free will, sin, and justification. At the last minute both parties backed away from their tentative rapprochement, and although no formal agreement was sustained, the Regensburg Colloquy remains a remarkable achievement of ecumenical dialogue.

After the failure to unite the empire theologically at Regensburg, Emperor Charles V imposed unity of a sort by military force, and by enforcing his own theological scheme, the Augsburg Interim of 1548. Bucer regarded this as a step against reform, and for his pains he was discharged from his pastorate in Strasbourg. He accepted an invitation from Archbishop Thomas Cranmer to settle in England. Even this brief sojourn in England at the end of his life left its continuing mark. Most notably, perhaps, was his influence on the *Second Prayer Book of Edward VI* (1552), as Cranmer's revision of the Anglican liturgy was called. Bucer's last great work, a treatise on Christian social ethics, *De Regno Christi*, his gift to Edward VI, was written after he was appointed Regius Professor of Divinity at Cambridge University. It was his contribution to the restitution of the kingdom of God in England.

Bucer died on the morning of March 1, 1551. The University of Cambridge accorded him an elaborate funeral in Great Saint Mary's Church. Yet four years later, when the religious currents had pulled in another direction, Queen Mary had his body exhumed and burned in public. Five years after that, the newly crowned Queen Elizabeth I attempted to redress the offense and ordered that Bucer should be restored to full honor, for which purpose a solemn assembly of state was held.

THEMES IN BUCER'S THEOLOGY

Bucer wrote no systematic theology in a manner similar to Calvin's *Institutes of the Christian Religion*. Rather, into his prolix Bible commentaries he inserted lengthy discussions on theological topics to which the texts under review gave rise. Theology by way of such reflections, *loci communes* or common places, was a practice of the day.[15] Thus his commentaries are more theological and homiletical than grammatical or philological. In his work he tried to be faithful to the total witness of scripture, searching always for dogmatic syntheses that would do justice to the diverse testimony.[16] Bucer wrote concerning the basis of all Christian doctrine that "nothing is to be taught unless it is either expressly set out in the Scriptures, or may be truly and certainly proved from the same."[17] This goal is amply illustrated in *On the True Pastoral Care*, with its many biblical citations.

Four broad areas of Bucer's theology are of interest in the study of his pastoral theology: (1) the doctrines of election and justification, (2) a noetic approach to the Word of God, (3) love as the corollary of faith, and (4) his eucharistic orientation.

Election and Justification

Election and justification shape the whole of Bucer's theology, and in particular his doctrine of election is notable for its sharp contours and consistency. He insists that salvation rests solely on God's sovereign choice and acts toward us in Jesus Christ.

> Almighty God takes pity on us, whom he has chosen for this purpose before the foundation of the world, purely in virtue of his free mercy and solely for the sake of his dear Son, and not because he was led to do so through any good works on our part, whether before or after we are born anew.[18]

The emphasis here is threefold: election is gracious, being the pure gift of God, and not a reward; election is restrictive, for only the elect will have faith; and the elect will participate in the order of salvation. The elect are called, justified, sanctified, and glorified.[19]

For Bucer, justification means both the imputation and the impartation of righteousness, and the two are not to be separated.[20] He appreciated the fact that God does not just forgive, but transforms the person who is forgiven to live an amended life. But even so, no person is so filled with good works that he or she never stands in need of the gracious forgiveness of God. The forgiveness of sins is not the end of justification, but instead is the beginning of a new relationship with God and of a life corresponding to it. Such a life demonstrates the sign of justification. Thus,

> by this interpretation, then, we elucidate our justification in terms of its special and primary effect, that of begetting virtues and good works. . . . That very righteousness and the good works wrought in us by the Spirit of Christ constitute the visible evidence of that unmerited acceptance of ours in the sight of God.[21]

In traditional language, then, Bucer holds very closely together the relation of sanctification to justification, for in justification a person is indeed united to Christ, becoming a partaker of his fruitfulness in good works. As a pastor-theologian Bucer was concerned not only with doctrinal considerations and right belief, but also with the life of his people before God.

The Word of God

Bucer advances a noetic approach to faith that is resolutely based on the Word of God heard through the grace and agency of the Holy Spirit. The natural ear cannot hear the Word of God. Matters of Christian faith, for example, must be rendered according to the Word of God and not according to human reason (*nit nach unser vernunfft, sonder nach dem wort Gottes*, 184, 2). For Bucer, no difference of meaning is apparent between *fides* and *credere*, between faith and belief.[22] Faith, wrote Bucer, is "an unwavering persuasion of God's mercy and fatherly kindness towards us . . . resting on the accepted sacrifice of Christ."[23] Faith is a knowing of Christ the Savior, carrying with it the "conviction of the expiation of sins and the conferring of life through the death and resurrection of Christ."[24] Faith, then, is not just trust, but also assent, an act of understanding and will:

> Thus hope and true reverence for God and love towards one's neighbour are certainly never absent from faith, but nevertheless faith itself is uniquely the faculty given to the saints by God, whereby they assent to his promises concerning the salvation accomplished for us through the Lord Jesus Christ.[25]

Such a view of faith reminds us again of the reason for understanding the minister in the Reformed tradition as the teaching elder.

Love

Love is, of course, faith's corollary. If faith has precedence over love from a Reformed perspective, love nevertheless follows immediately. Torrance comments upon Bucer's "amazingly eschatological conception of *love* that is the most moving and characteristic element in (his) theology."[26] Loving care and service of others is as much a mark of Bucer's last works as they are of his first,[27] for his belief was consistent that faith does not stand alone, but is active in deeds of love, and where love is absent, faith also is absent.[28] Love is Bucer's characteristic mark of sanctification and the sign of the indwelling of the Holy Spirit.

At times, especially when writing on church discipline, Bucer can sound harsh. This tone is mitigated significantly when we recall how deeply he understood the living of the Christian life as a life of love. In fact, Bucer argued that in Christian love each member of the body of Christ is to serve others. Christian love is a love that always turns away from oneself and towards others; because the Christian is, by definition, secure in Christ, he or she need take no heed for himself or herself. As such, however, Christian love is not mere altruism, but is the good work towards and for others that is God's will for them. As the primary fruit of the Spirit, after faith, love is to guide all gifts of the Spirit.

The Eucharist

Bucer's eucharistic orientation not only shaped his theology but also motivated much of his involvement in the politics of reform, as we have seen. From at least after 1528, and after becoming convinced that Luther's treatment was in agreement with his own and Zwingli's, "nothing so possessed him, heart and soul, as the pursuit of a Protestant concord on the Supper."[29] Like a theological metaphor straddling the Rhine, between Zwinglian Switzerland and Lutheran Germany, Bucer's Strasbourg represented a mediating position on the Lord's Supper.[30] The issue was whether Christ was figuratively or in some way substantially present in the elements of the Holy Communion. Both sides could claim Bucer at different times. As to Bucer's own view, his mature position, written in his *Brief Summary of Christian Doctrine* in 1548, holds out both a material and spiritual, or an earthly and a heavenly, aspect: Christ does not leave heaven, neither is he mingled with the elements, nor locally confined in them. Rather, Christ gives himself to us "after a heavenly manner," as food and sustenance for eternal life. He calls this a "simple and scriptural confession" and warns against meddling in "inopportune contention" that serves only to confound the truth.[31]

ON THE TRUE PASTORAL CARE

Von der waren Seelsorge was published in Strasbourg in April 1538, at the request of his fellow pastors in the church at Strasbourg (*seiner mitarbiter am wort des Herren in der Kirchen zu Strassburg*, 241, 5), as the seal at the end of the manuscript puts it. This note suggests that his goal was pastoral and practical, being an account of the practice of ministry whereby the church may escape schism and division and find instead a true unity and good order in Christ and through his word. The book shows above all else that Bucer was a theologian because he was a pastor, every bit as much as he was a pastor because he was a theologian. In literal translation its full title is: *On the true pastoral care and the correct shepherd-service, how this is to be established and carried out in the Church of Christ* (90.1). Bucer wrote the book out of the conviction that pastors were losing their way in the care of souls and people were reluctant anymore to submit to the yoke of Christ. Like the classical texts already discussed, Bucer's was written for the purpose of reforming the ministry. On two fronts, from the Roman Church and from the leaders of Protestant sects, Bucer felt that the true church of Christ was under attack. This "little book," as he called it, was an attempt to restore a proper understanding of the church of Christ with regard to order and ministry, with an especial concern for faithful pastoral care that leads to the salvation of Christ's people (94, 13f). To this end his intent was not to omit anything that leads to godly discipline in the administration of the church.

Bucer used scripture as the foundation for everything he wanted to say, as the Lord gave him insight. The theme verse for his book is taken from Ezekiel 34:16, which is cited in his brief introduction: "I will seek the lost, and I will bring back the strayed, and I will bind up the injured, and I will strengthen the weak, but the fat and the strong I will destroy. I will feed them with justice" (93, 1f).[32]

Two aspects of Bucer's pastoral theology bear critically on the practice of pastoral care today: his biblical and christological emphases, and his understanding of the broad tasks of pastoral care, with special emphases on evangelism and pastoral discipline understood as submitting to the yoke of Christ.

Biblical and Christological Emphases

Two dominant themes in Bucer's approach are evident at all points: the role of the Bible in his pastoral theological method and a thoroughgoing christological focus in which Bucer displays a remarkable awareness of the active personal rule of Jesus Christ in and over his church. In both regards Bucer stands over and against much contemporary writing in pastoral theology.

As with his theology in general, Bucer's pastoral theology is an extended commentary on selected scriptural passages. He operated within a conventional Reformation approach to scripture. Authority comes from the Holy Spirit, the key agent in scripture's writing and interpretation. Bucer allowed no separation between scripture and the Holy Spirit. In the power of the Spirit the Bible alone is authoritative in all matters concerning salvation. Nothing is to be taught in the church concerning God that is not directly set forth in scripture, or that may be deduced clearly from it. This caveat extends to cover the practice of the church in all regards. But that something can be found in the Bible is not enough. The Bible is not self-referencing: it is about Christ.[33] Scripture and Christology thus belong together.

The theme text is, as was noted, the sheepfold metaphor from Ezekiel 34:16. Taking his paradigm from this verse, he identifies the five tasks of the care of souls: searching for the lost; bringing back the strays; binding up the wounded sheep (that is, those who have fallen into sin); strengthening the weak; and guarding and feeding the healthy sheep. Even if this fivefold pattern does not quite fit with a contemporary presentation of the text from Ezekiel, the schema still stands as a worthy goal of pastoral care that is biblical in a deep and powerful sense.

Each chapter of *Von der waren Seelsorge* begins with a series of cited biblical passages that Bucer comments upon in realist fashion, and from which he moves into didactic pastoral theological reflection. Scholarly exegesis, theological reflection, and the practice of Christian ministry form a tightly woven fabric throughout. At all points his approach is expositional and deductive, attending not only to the letter of scripture, but also to its true spirit and the power of the Lord (*waren geyst und kraft des Herren*, 98, 4). Thus, the emphasis always moves on to Christ's lordship over the church through the various ministries. Christ, alive and reigning—not scripture—has and exercises all power and rule in the church and congregation. So Bucer emphasizes that the Christian life is lived "in Christ," who is our dear Lord, to whom all things must be subordinated

(*unserem lieben Herren, dem wir alles ander nachsetzen*, 98, 12). By this understanding Christ is served by means of his word.

Bucer's biblical emphasis is in direct contrast with much contemporary
pastoral theology. So little exegesis or biblical theology appears within the
pages of many current texts that one must wonder if biblical studies have
any relevance for many teachers of pastoral care. Modern pastoral theology is characterized largely by the study of what Anton T. Boisen, the
founder of the Clinical Pastoral Education movement in the United
States, called "living human documents"—that is, the study of people,
especially in their distress—rather than the study of biblical texts. Consequently, the lack of scripture and the dominance of psychology have been
marked features in pastoral care literature over the last seventy years.

The limited use of scripture in pastoral theology is illustrated in the
many writings of Seward Hiltner, the leading figure in the formation of
the modern pastoral care movement in the United States since the 1950s.
Hiltner's inductive approach, following Boisen, saw the study of pastoral
events and human experiences as the primary fonts of constructive theological inquiry. Hiltner secondarily advocated a mutual critical correlation
between biblical and classical theology and reflection on pastoral experience, but his practice betrayed his formal method. According to Hiltner,
the meaning of shepherding or pastoral care is given in the parable of the
Good Samaritan (Luke 10:25–37). As such, this approach involves individualized care directed towards healing, sustaining, or guiding, whatever
the circumstance calls for, without regard for larger groups or institutions.
When Hiltner fills out what he intends, however, he employs psy-
chotherapeutic, largely Rogerian, categories to interpret human experience and pastoral practice. Biblical categories immediately give way to
pastoral counseling theory and drop out of sight.[34]

A few recent writers on pastoral care have urged a turn to a more biblical approach to pastoral care,[35] yet little foundational connection exists
between pastoral theology and biblical studies in much pastoral care literature today. Even so, the lack of scripture as such is not the primary concern to raise here but rather its consequence: the eclipse of Jesus Christ
from pastoral care.

Bucer's overriding concern is for the relationship of humankind to God
that is effected in Jesus Christ and to which the ministry of the gospel bears
witness. The goal of true pastoral care, according to Bucer, is that Christians may know that Christ alone has all power and rule in his church (*das
Christus unser Herre allen gewalt und regierung in seiner Kirchen*, 105.3);
Christ feeds his people, cares for them, brings in those who are lost,
watches over them, and leads and provides for them so that they may grow

in holiness (105, 3f). Christ is truly and actively alive in the church, according to Bucer, not in a tangible or worldly way, for he is in heaven, but as a king over his kingdom, as a master with his disciples, as a shepherd caring for the flock, as a bridegroom with his bride, and as a doctor with the sick (105, 14f). In this way Bucer builds everything upon his understanding of the personal authority and rule of Christ as an active reality through the Holy Spirit in the life of the church. This emphasis is important, for Christ here is not understood or presented as a cosmic principle or a moral force, but as the living personal presence of God with us.

In a remarkable chapter (number three in the German edition), Bucer outlines the christological basis for and the authority of pastoral work. He writes that the Lord Jesus carries out his pastoral or shepherd office (*sein hirtenampt*) and the work of salvation through the office of the ministry (107, 22). This important point can easily be missed. All ministry is Christ's ministry of ruling, leading, protecting, caring, and feeding the church, in which ministry of Christ the ministries of the church participate. The apostles are to make disciples for the Lord and baptize them; the Lord brings people to salvation through the preaching of repentance and forgiveness of sins; the ministers of the Word are empowered to bear fruit, that is, people's salvation and their access to heaven. Thus the Lord empowers his ministers through the Holy Spirit to bring people into faith, and to write himself on their hearts. In this manner, Jesus Christ makes people Christian and blesses them through the ministry of the church (*Der Herr machet die leut Christen und selig durch den Kirchendienst*, 109, 32). By such a divine condescension the ministry of the church is vital if the work of redemption is to penetrate deeply into people's hearts, although the power and authority always belongs not to the ministers of the gospel but to Jesus Christ.

We found a similar pastoral theology earlier in the writings of Gregory of Nazianzus and John Chrysostom, in their comments on the priest as the soul of the congregation and through whom the Lord Jesus draws people up to himself. Bucer's language is different, and his conceptual framework is not that of Greek metaphysics. But a theological similarity undergirds all these texts insofar as the work of ministry in each case is given such soteriological significance and authority. Each writer argues that the task of the ministry of the church is to preach and teach the Word of God, and to care for the people with the power of Christ's love for them, and thus they may come to a sure knowledge of their salvation.

Bucer, apparently, had little interest in the kind of intrapsychic concerns and practices that dominate pastoral work today, as helpful as they are in their proper place. His focus, rather, is christological and evangelical in the sense that the love of Jesus Christ and the relationship of a person before God dominate his concerns—the true salvation of Christ's lambs, as he states again and again. The stark singularity of this christological emphasis is the mark of true pastoral care.

Such christological considerations in pastoral care are rare insofar as most modern pastoral writers, following Schleiermacher, Boisen, and Hiltner, tend towards an inductive, experience-based approach that lends itself to a creative engagement with psychology but stands counter to Bucer's classical, biblically based christological approach.[36] Without minimizing the benefit of psychology for pastoral work today, the question of what makes pastoral care Christian must arise. Howard Clinebell, for example, a leading writer on pastoral care over the past thirty years, in his influential *Basic Types of Pastoral Care and Counseling*, argues that a spiritual dimension must be present in pastoral care.[37] Quite so! But what he means by this remains unclear, and the statement itself contributes nothing to the Christian identity of pastoral care. While people talk of wholeness and growth, certainly, as the meaning of spiritual care, as one reviewer noted "one hears a great deal about the spiritual, but remarkably little about Christ—or even about the Holy Spirit."[38] The observation could be extended to cover much of the field. With the loss of the christological emphasis in much pastoral theology today has come a corresponding loss of the true nature of the pastoral office and of its concomitant authority. The centrality of Jesus Christ in his understanding of the Christian life controls Bucer's identification of the tasks of the pastoral office.

The Scope of Pastoral Care

For Bucer, as we have seen, Jesus Christ alone has and exercises all power and rule in the church, for he rules, feeds, and cares for it, and through the church Christ brings the gospel to those people who are lost or have stayed away from the ways of God. He does this in order that his flock may be purified more thoroughly and liberated from sin and sin's consequences. Bucer's goal is that God's people may be saved and encouraged to grow in piety and blessedness. He notes two goals of the pastoral office that ministers exercise on behalf of Christ: the first is evangelism, whereby those whom God has chosen to be part of Christ's flock, but who are not yet in the sheepfold, are brought in; the second is the care of those who have already been brought in so that they may continue to grow in godliness (116, 31f). Pastoral work consists of seeking the lost and guiding the faithful through ministries of teaching, exhorting, warning, disciplining, comforting, pardoning, and reconciling people to God. Different epochs of the church's life have emphasized one function as the organizing task around which the others revolved.[39] The Reformation is characterized by reconciliation as the dominant pastoral feature.[40] A main theme of *Von der waren Seelsorge* is a presentation of the processes of pastoral reconciliation, first for the lost and strayed, that they be brought back to their Lord, but also for people within the fellowship whose sin must be addressed.

We will consider the evangelistic responsibility of pastoral work first, and then turn to the tasks of pastoral care for those who are within the discipline of the church.

Pastoral Care as Evangelism and Reconciliation

The evangelical heart of Bucer's theology leads him to see evangelism as a primary feature of pastoral care, an evangelism directed both to those who have not yet heard and responded to the word of Christ the Lord, as well as to those who have been part of the body of Christ but who have fallen away. Not only are the lost sheep to be sought, but also the stayed sheep are to be restored. In such a way, according to Bucer, pastoral care must have as a primary responsibility a concern for the salvation of the sinners lost and strayed who are still God's elect.

In considering pastoral care as an evangelistic ministry, a brief highlighting of Bucer's understanding of sin, election, and salvation would be helpful. "Sin," he wrote in his *Commentary on Romans*, "is the scriptural name for our going astray by forsaking the only God, who is man's highest good, in order to pursue unsubstantial and ruinous phantoms of the good."[41] Sin, thus, is a radical subversion of our human personhood, making us incapable of desiring and doing what is good. Election, for Bucer, means that in God's sovereign choice and mercy, some people are called out of sin, and to that end are justified, sanctified, and glorified. In Bucer's theology, election means first that human works do not have any role to play in our salvation, and and second, salvation depends upon God's free work on our behalf in Christ.[42] The various marks and contexts of the elect form a subplot in Bucer's pastoral theology, shaping as they do the condition of the sheep and the nature of the pastoral response. To Bucer, justification cannot be separated from sanctification or vocation, for God not only transforms a person's standing before God—imputing righteousness—but also transforms a person's life, leading to right living and acting in the world—imparting righteousness.[43] Thus God sends us through the ministry of the Gospel both the grace won for us through the suffering and death of Jesus, and the Holy Spirit, to bring us to a true, complete, and sincere belief in this Gospel.

With regard to the lost sheep, Bucer insists and then repeats that pastoral evangelism is to be pursued with the highest diligence and unremitting effort (144, 23) by the faithful servants of Christ. Thus, faithfulness to God's command demands that ministers must miss no one with the word of salvation in order to bring the elect into Christ's sheepfold, and he highlights Mark 16:15, "'Go into all the world and proclaim the good news to the whole creation.'" People, in fact, he argues, are to be compelled or forced (*notigen*) into the kingdom of Christ, citing Luke 14:21–23 as the authority (144, 5). Bucer means that Christians are to be so persistent and urgent in pressing the gospel that evil people experience evangelism to be a compulsion. The job is not complete until people who are called by God to faith have entered into the communion of Christ.

Note Bucer's emphasis that all Christians, and not just pastors, are to be pastoral evangelists. For ministers who fail in the evangelical task, Bucer has harsh words, and in support he cites Ezekiel 34:4. The Lord has appointed ministers in his church to seek the salvation of the lost. Christ will require at their hands the blood of the lambs not brought to him (*ir blut würdt der Herr von deren henden erfordren*, 154, 5). This accountability to God for the faithful exercise of ministry, as we have noted already, is a theme found in all of the texts representing the classical tradition in pastoral theology. Its repeated use throughout the tradition should alert us to its cardinal importance.

Not just the lost, however, but also the stray sheep—who having once been with Christ but who through false doctrine or the wiles of the flesh have lost their way—must with an even greater diligence on the pastor's part be restored to the fellowship of the church, as a matter of pastoral urgency. Bucer interprets Luke 15:4–6, from the parable of the Lost Sheep, to mean that whatever is necessary must be done as a matter of highest priority in order to win back for Christ people who once acknowledged him and are still his. Imaginatively, Bucer uses Galatians 4:19–20 to interpret the meaning of the effort involved. The work of restoring the wayward to the communion of Christ is likened to an anguished childbirth (156, 18). Describing those pastors who go in search for Christ's lost lambs, Bucer uses a striking series of images: they leave everything to search for, find, and bring home the persons who have wandered from Christ; they do this not only by direction or coercion, but also by carrying them home on their shoulders; and like mothers, in a sense, they give birth again, with much pain, though also with great gentleness (157, 3f).

The grounding of evangelism in pastoral care gives it a historical home. Pastoral theologians should certainly not be too possessive at this point. Yet whatever else must be said regarding evangelism, as a ministry of the church it remains an expression of God's care for the salvation of Christ's lambs. However, as Brooks Holifield has shown, the history of pastoral care in North America is marked precisely by the movement away from the concern for salvation to the concern for self-realization.[44] This shift represents a serious problem. On the one hand, evangelism is cut off from pastoral work, with the result that it is pushed out to the margins of ministry, as if it were an elective in the curriculum of ministry. An uncertainty concerning the need for and the nature of evangelism is a feature of mainline European and North American Protestantism today. On the other hand, pastoral work itself, without an evangelistic imperative, becomes trivialized, concerned increasingly only with care and not with salvation. Pastoral care loses its soteriological and eschatological goal. Bucer speaks an urgent word to pastors today to return with diligence to a pastoral practice that is built upon the whole Word of God, and which is thereby both evangelical in theology and evangelistic in practice.

Pastoral Care as Pastoral Discipline

Bucer turns then to the pastoral care of those who are within the communion of Christ. Half of *Von the waren Seelsorge* is devoted to this topic, and he gives a significant amount of space to the pastoral care of gross and notorious sinners—that is, people who turn away from Christ, disobey those in authority, engage in serious misbehavior against others, or are prey to immoderate habits. Thus the second major emphasis after evangelism in his discussion of the scope of pastoral care is pastoral discipline, and Bucer's discussion is singular and remarkable because of the significance he affords it.

As the sacrament of confession was abandoned by the Protestants at the Reformation, the task fell upon the pastors and elders, through home visitation, to assist people in their personal lives of faith at the point where sin, especially habitual sin, had to be confronted. Bucer begins in a low-key manner, expressing the view, from Matthew 18:15–17, that anyone who sins is to be corrected by a neighbor, or, if necessary by the congregation (157, 15). His schoolmasterish tone should not allow us to fail to see that the goal is reconciliation to God and the joy of communion with God. Bucer's underlying reason for pastoral discipline is that for one to live in sin is to live opposed to God, to be wounded. Bucer reflects the Reformation's concerns to take sin seriously as an impediment to new life in Christ and to the proclamation of the forgiveness of sins as the basis for the Christian life. He nuances this stand with his serious concern for the need for penance on the part of sinners as the way in which sin is rooted out.

Bucer devoted much space in *Von der waren Seelsorge* to his consideration of pastoral discipline, and proportionately less space to his consideration of pastoral care of the weak and the healthy who are to be guarded.

Bucer makes three introductory points concerning *pastoral discipline*: (a) it is the responsibility of all Christians, to care for sinners, as noted above, but the pastor has an especial responsibility (159, 4f and 18f); (b) attempts to bind up and heal the wounds caused by sin should continue for as long as a sinner accepts the voice of the pastor (159, 24f); and (c) the treatment to heal the wounded parishioner should enable him or her to acknowledge the sin and be moved to true contrition and sorrow, to the end that the person is comforted and strengthened in hope of grace (159, 36f). With Christ as the source, the process for dealing with sin sounds remarkably contemporary. Neither judgment from without nor the imposition of punishment brings healing, but the personal realization whereby one names for oneself: "I have sinned, and I desire grace." Bringing a person to such self-awareness requires, says Bucer, a gentle spirit and great love (160, 19), so much so that one must be prepared even to bear the sinner's burden oneself. Here Bucer follows Paul, who believed that he might have to bear the humiliation himself if sinners had failed to do so (2 Cor. 12:21). In this way, believers share not only in one another's joy, but also in their suffering. Penance is serious and must be practiced with moderation; the goals are renewal of life and faith, not punishment and despair. The danger is always that an undue or immoderate penitential burden may lead a person to leave the church or be plunged into despair. Great wisdom is needed by a pastor who guides a penitent along the path of amendment of life, and frequently Bucer describes these pastors as "faithful shepherds," implying perhaps that faithfulness is not a designation appropriate to all.

Bucer, citing Martin Luther, says the issue is whether we really want to be Christians, in view of the fact that we keep sinning (193, 28). If our answer is Yes, we need to listen to Christ and purge our sins, especially the greater sins, for they wound us deeply. Lesser sins may be dealt with by daily confession and repentance, but for serious sins, saying, "I am sorry, and I won't do it again" is not enough (172, 28), for an outward show of piety and repentance can mask an inward resistance. A deeper response is called for, one that will root out the source of sin. Bucer suggests that true repentance in fact is associated with weeping and lamenting, much praying, and fasting and self-discipline. Excluding a person from the Lord's Table may even be necessary when he or she is bound to a period of penance because of serious sin. Satisfaction is not the goal, however, but the prevention of present and future sins. Penitence is not an atoning work, but a process in sanctification and the amendment of life. Coming to a true knowledge of one's sins—as far as that is possible for us—leads to deep regret and profound repentance.

Bucer rooted his support for the necessity of penitential discipline in the Bible and the early church. While he cites Old Testament examples, he relies primarily on the treatment of the Corinthian sinner (1 Cor. 5:1–5) to show that penance is God's command. The casting out of a sinner from the community, however, is mitigated by forgiveness in due course, lest the sinner be overwhelmed by excessive sorrow (2 Cor. 2:7), a sorrow so deep, perhaps, that it leads to a depression. In any case, Bucer regarded penitential discipline as the Lord's command, through the Holy Spirit, who orders the church (170, 17f). He calls it both "this order and correction of Christ" (*ordnung und zucht Christi*, 195, 24), and "a work and command of Christ" (*eyn werck und befelch Christi*, 197, 30). Without discipline, sin runs amok, yet as Christ's sheep, sinners listen to his voice.

Pastoral discipline is potentially dangerous for everyone. For the pastor, its practice can encourage authoritarian and intrusive modes of ministry, as occurred in Scotland, for example, in the centuries following the Reformation when ministers and elders acted more like moral police officers than loving shepherds of Christ's flock. Discipline is dangerous for parishioners when it becomes narrow and hardened. Degenerating into a deadening legalism that kills rather than quickens faith, discipline can cause fear of God rather than love for Christ. Pastoral discipline, the process of enabling repentance and penitence, must be exercised in love, with humility, and as an operation of grace designed to win people back to faithfulness.

Bucer did not have modern psychological insights to guide him. He saw sin for what he believed it was and what it is: an offense to God that can be rooted out by the means of grace and the care of Christian pastors and friends. To that end he saw a place for the instruction and admonition of the Word of God, personally accepted mortifications, and, in the case of serious sins, exclusion of the sinner from the Lord's Supper until life was amended. Today we are able to appreciate that sin involves more than the failure of moral will and attack by the devil. Also involved are issues of human development and moral formation, the inadequacy of which renders one less able to act with discernment and responsibility. Moreover, social, political, and economic factors can malform people and societies, enable sin in institutional and corporate contexts, and trap people in behavior patterns from which they can hardly escape. Nevertheless, we should focus attention on choices evilly made and acted upon, and on continuing patterns of belief and behavior that fall short of God's will for our lives. Many of us are not helpless victims, and personal responsibility must come to bear. The issue is not always mental health but is always sanctification, which is the reason for pastoral discipline.

Bucer turns briefly to consider the pastoral care of the weak and the healthy members of the church. The proportionate lack of space given to this in comparison to pastoral discipline indicates where he saw his priority. We need not follow him in this, and modern practice has almost entirely not done so. Yet this emphasis alone allows us to see a lacuna in pastoral practice today. The tendency of much contemporary pastoral care is to emphasize a God who cares,[45] often to the exclusion of God's judgment on sin as an issue to be addressed in people's lives. Pastoral theologians today, on the whole, have tended to avoid discussion of sin altogether or to see it as a developmental problem requiring treatment.[46] Bucer reminds us that, while the need for pastoral counseling as a form of psychotherapy is not at all an inappropriate focus for pastoral care, the issue of persons standing before God at the point of their sin is still crucial and that we, pastors and people together, neglect confronting this issue at our peril.

Bucer turns finally to *pastoral care of the weak and the healthy*. Bucer had a largely cognitive understanding of human weaknesses: those weaknesses, he believes, come from insufficiency of faith and stupidity with respect to faith and the fear of God (208, 6). The weak have become timid and do not hold on to Christ firmly enough. Their knowledge of Jesus Christ and the Christian life is inadequate, and their hold on the will of Christ for their lives remains insecure. Because deeper faith and correction come from the Word of God (209, 17), people depend upon this Word being carefully given to them. Bucer's pastoral care in this regard is largely didactic.

While no one is perfect, the healthy sheep of the flock are those nonetheless who live in fear of God, stay within the fellowship of the church, and live the Christian life (214, 9). In a typically Reformation teaching, Bucer insists that the goal of pastoral care to the healthy is to assist them in being built up in Christ and thus in his grace, who has called them into his kingdom and glory (215, 7). Growth in Christian life comes, Bucer argues, through proper teaching, admonition, and counsel. Again the approach to pastoral care is didactic. This care is performed both corporately and privately, in the church from the pulpit, and in people's homes face-to-face (217, 26). In this way the doctrine of Christ is applied generally to everybody, but also personally to each case. Care of the healthy sheep also involves protecting them from those who would infect the body with their evil ways and who have no wish to repent and reform. Bucer has no qualms about excommunicating people for the sake of the congregation's health.

This ministry of care is above all else a ministry of love (224, 13). Neither being domineering (*herrisch*) nor unfriendly, the caregiver is to act humbly and like a mother (*muterlich*), like a nurse with her child (225, 11). This series of words to describe the appropriate attitude to take in pastoral care is most interesting, suggesting that ministry is here at least construed in feminine rather than masculine terms.

On a critical note, the extent to which Bucer's concept of pastoral work is rooted in the proclamation of the gospel, while a marked strength, makes it open to the kind of rejection that has been found appropriate to lay before the approach of Eduard Thurneysen, whose classically styled *Theology of Pastoral Care* represents a so-called Barthian emphasis.[47] Along with Thurneysen, Bucer falls prey to a kind of homiletical reductionism of pastoral care, stressing pastoral work as proclamation, teaching, and admonition to such an extent that it becomes preaching writ small. The issue may be more formal than material, however. Pastors have ways to present the evangelical content of the gospel without always speaking at people. Surely the content of the gospel may be communicated, along with preaching and teaching, in acts of love clearly explained, in relationships by which suffering is shared and borne, and in which healing is provided. Not the least of what comes to mind is the recovery of a liturgical dimension to pastoral care, in which the love of Christ is expressed through confession and absolution, anointing and blessing, Eucharist and prayer in common. Bucer's point, in the end, is that pastoral care is to be informed through and through by the gospel of Jesus Christ as the living Word of God, and that the content of God's grace in Jesus Christ gives pastoral work an inevitable evangelical and, indeed, evangelistic, dimension.

Both generally as a theologian and reformer, and specifically as a pastoral theologian, Martin Bucer remains largely undiscovered and therefore unknown by the modern church. His legacy and contribution to pastoral work today is perhaps as an *agent provocateur*, one who may be slipped into the discussion on the nature of pastoral care to help us see from a different perspective and thereby to uncover matters now rather long overlooked. His pastoral care was tailored to another age. Yet his insistence that the focus of pastoral care is the life of persons before God in Jesus Christ is for us both a word of judgment on a discipline that has become concerned largely only with inward states, as it is an opportunity to reform a most noble and holy occupation according to the Word of God.

5

Richard Baxter,
The Reformed Pastor

I Preach'd, as never sure to Preach again
And as a dying man to dying men.

Poetical Fragments

It is but the least part of a Minister's work, which is done in the
Pulpit.

The Saints' Everlasting Rest

I know not what it doth by others; but the most Reverend Preacher,
that speaks as if he saw the face of God, doth more affect my heart,
though with common words, than an unreverent man with the
most exquisite preparations.

The Reformed Pastor

Richard Baxter's *The Reformed Pastor* is still in print after 350 years, which
is an astonishing accomplishment for a long-winded and poorly edited
book, written by an English Puritan whose method of pastoral care
appears to be an exercise in compulsive overwork and a recipe for exhaustion. The reason for its long life is simple: in spite of its and Baxter's shortcomings, the book bears witness to the nature and power of pastoral
ministry perhaps more convincingly that any other book in the history of
pastoral literature.

That claim is not too large to make. For many generations, pastors have
drawn upon this book for both practical wisdom and spiritual inspiration.
They have found in its pages a call to self-examination that probes to the
quick and an encouragement for renewed dedication to their godly work.
The book presents a remarkable synthesis of biblical theology and well-
tested, practical application, which while written in the context of its time,

still has force and conviction for pastors many centuries later. It is a testimony to the Puritan dictum that theological truth is for practice. *The Reformed Pastor* is still a text for this time, to be read by anybody concerned for the renewal of ministry. The title page of the original edition printed the word "Reformed" larger than any other to indicate the basic theme— namely, the book's call for the revived or renewed pastor, for only a renewed pastor can revive a sleeping congregation.

A BRIEF HISTORY OF PURITANISM

English Puritanism began as a reform movement within the Church of England, which was formed by Henry VIII in response in part to the Catholic Mary's reign of terror. Puritanism began during the reign of Elizabeth I (1558–1603) and sought, for about a century, to fight for the Protestant point of view in order to complete the work begun during the English Reformation. Puritanism was a heterogeneous movement, which while broadly Calvinist, was diverse in doctrine, church polity, and civil politics; yet it was united in an effort to conform church and society to a godly—that is, a biblical and evangelical—purity. Largely a clergy-led movement, Puritanism was characterized in spite of its diversity by beliefs concerning the authority of the Bible, the affirmation of Calvinism, the reform of the worship of the Church of England, and a profound conviction regarding the need to evangelize the mind as the way into renewing the heart.

In a narrow sense, and illustrative of its defining ethos, English Puritanism arose in direct response to a third Act of Uniformity (1559), following the murderous Catholic interlude of Mary I. This act reestablished the use of the *Second Prayer Book* (1552); it also included an "ornaments rubric" commanding clergy to wear the surplice and cope and other Roman vestments during the celebration of Holy Communion. Many clergy felt they could not comply, for fear of being so closely associated with the Mass. The vestments symbolized all that had been fought against and suffered under amid exile or execution during the Catholic terror. The subsequent vestments controversy reveals the ideals of the nascent Puritanism awakened thereby in the English church. How could the church so easily and quickly adopt Roman practices when the blood of the Protestant martyrs had not yet seeped into the soil of England? The Puritans wanted a complete break with all Roman practices. As the *Admonition* of 1572 made clear, true reformation consisted in "abandoning all popish remnants both in ceremonies and in regiment," and "also in bringing in and placing in God's Church those things only which the Lord Himself in His Word commandeth."[1] Along with the refusal to wear vestments, many Puritans refused to kneel at the Lord's Supper or use the sign of the cross at baptism, for lack of biblical warrant.

Elizabeth would brook no dissent from her clergy. Although the Church of England was evenly balanced between "Catholic" and "Protestant" influences, Elizabeth called for compliance with her policies. Puritan clergymen began to be suspended or imprisoned; some fled to Presbyterian Scotland or beyond. In 1572, the Puritans appealed to Parliament for relief from the burden of law. Their manifesto, *Admonition*, outraged the queen, for she feared that a political agenda threatening the royal supremacy lay behind the theological presentation. In reality, reform was badly needed. The church was in a deplorable state: absentee, inefficient, and ignorant ministers at the very least called the faithfulness of the church into question. Separatist and reforming viewpoints grew side by side, the former especially meeting with interference and punishment, and in some cases execution. The government's Conventicle Act of 1593 was intended to defeat separatism once and for all, imposing imprisonment and even banishment to people who did not attend the Church of England. From this circumstance, many Puritans fled to Holland; a number of these exiles became the *Mayflower* pilgrims in 1620, bringing their Puritanism with them to the New World.

In 1603 James I (VI of Scotland, the son of Mary, Queen of Scots, and who had held the Scottish throne since 1567) succeeded Elizabeth. All parties looked to him with hope: the Catholics because of his mother, the Presbyterian Puritans because of his Scottish upbringing, and the Anglicans because of his known antipathy to Presbyterianism. The Puritan party pleaded for toleration, but church and king demanded obedience, setting the Puritans and the government in opposition. In 1625, after Charles succeeded his father, events move rapidly out of control. Religious and political dissenters joined forces in a civil war against both the monarch and the established church (led by Archbishop William Laud). Charles and his political and ecclesiastical lieutenants were executed and the Puritans, led by Oliver Cromwell, were in power from 1648 until 1660. With the Restoration in 1660, Charles II purged the Puritans from the Church of England, although they survived as dissenting communities, forming Baptist, Congregational, and Presbyterian congregations. When the "glorious revolution" of 1688 brought William and Mary to the throne, these free churches were granted toleration.

English historian Hugh Martin identifies the essence of Puritanism as lying in three foundational principles: "1. A belief in the reality and audibility of God's voice in the Bible and in the contemporaneous work of the Holy Spirit. 2. A conviction of the need to worship God in the beauty of holiness. 3. A keen sense of responsibility to God for oneself and for other men."[2] Certainly the sense of a people discovering the power of the Bible for the first time in their mother tongue and with the sense of being personally addressed by God through its pages motivated the Puritans to a conviction concerning God and an intensity of Christian life and worship that was singular in English history to this point. Their view of Christian faith meant, too, a rejection of all that was not prescribed in scripture: kneeling at Holy Communion, the sign of the cross at Baptism, pagan names for children, and so on.

The Puritans rejected church tradition as mere Roman accretion. For moderates and sacramentarians in the Church of England, this approach implied a rigorous biblical dispensationalism that undercut the agency of the Holy Spirit in the life and history of the church. They argued instead for an understanding of the Bible and tradition, in which both were understood to be the work of the Holy Spirit. The Puritans resorted on occasion to biblical proof-texting, which was often narrow and extreme in perspective. But compared with the moral laxity, theological ignorance, and constitutional confusion that abounded throughout the Church of England, Puritanism implied a reform of, and the injection of seriousness of Christian purpose into, church and state. But for any of this to happen, reforming private life would be necessary.

RICHARD BAXTER: A BRIEF BIOGRAPHY

Baxter was born on November 12, 1615, into a moderately wealthy family. He was a big man, capable of forcing his personality and size upon any person or situation. While peaceable in intention, he tended to be combative, quick to judgment, and didactic in style. These traits made him a poor performer in public life. His outspokenness and his attitude of triumphalism, which were motivated by his convictions of conscience, rarely led to his desired result, for he tended to speak down to people. Yet as a pastoral evangelist he is without equal, perhaps because he had a passionate heart for the unconverted and was utterly committed to a teaching ministry, the primary characteristics of his pastoral work.[3]

Baxter was sickly throughout his life, and from puberty on believed he was always on the point of death. He had good reason to think so. He had smallpox when he was fourteen years old, and later experienced chronic colds, nosebleeds, and spitting of blood. Throughout his adult life he suffered from chronic intestinal illness (which he attributed to eating too much stolen fruit as a child!) and pains "as if I had been daily fill'd with wind." His blood was like "thin ink," and hemorrhages continued through his eyes and gums. He suffered from chronic eye disease, almost losing sight in one eye. Needless to say, he had "terrible toothache." He had recurring kidney stones. In sum, "very terrible" pains accompanied him throughout his life. His attempted cures have a humorous side. He liked to sit by roaring fires and to exercise "till I sweat." But most curiously, he would drink "beer as hot as my throat will endure, drunk all at once, to make me sweat."[4] Sheep milk brought him "the greatest increase of my Ease, Strength and Flesh, of anything that ever I tried." A mass in his throat caused him much concern—"hard as a Bone, and about as big as a . . . small Button," which he "too oft looked at in the Glass," fearing cancer. This medical emergency he believed that prayers cured.[5] His constant illness had "a great operation" upon his soul,[6] however, giving him a sense both of urgency in ministry and mercy from God. The epigram that heads this essay, from *Poetical Fragments*, which he often cited, indicates that he was driven not to despair but rather to make the best possible use of his time.

This account of his health concerns raises the question of the extent to which Baxter's own experience of illness, sense of vulnerability, and dependence upon God sharpened his pastoral sensibilities and empowerment, in a manner comparable perhaps to Paul in 2 Corinthians 1:3f. Baxter himself noted that "in all my labours at Kidderminster (where he was pastor), after my return (from the army, in which he served as a chaplain during the Civil War) I did all under languishing weakness, being seldom an hour free from pain."[7] His ministry certainly carried an urgent edge, as *The Reformed Pastor* makes clear, no doubt attributable in part to his sickness.

His father was a convert—called a "Puritan" as a term of derision because of his reading of the Bible on Sunday—who introduced the youngster to the Bible, "drawing me on to love the Bible and to search by degrees into the rest."[8] In time, divinity came to occupy "the first and chiefest place"[9] in his studies: "nothing can be rightly known, if God be not known."[10]

He was never formally educated, though from an early age showed scholarly ability. He was a private student under the guidance of the notable Puritan theologian John Owen. The English historian Geoffrey Nuttall comments that he was "an eager, sensitive, intelligent boy; lovable, but perhaps rather lonely."[11] Baxter was ordained deacon in 1638 and served briefly as a curate and schoolteacher before being called in March 1641 to the parish of Kidderminster, where he served until the

Restoration in 1660. His ministry there was almost immediately inter-rupted, however, for he was compelled to leave Kidderminster, a royalist town (for Gloucester, and later for Coventry), because of his (reluctant) support for Parliament and the Puritan cause. Although by temperament and conviction—though not by manner, as we have seen—he was a man who sought moderation and unity rather than division (later he would be condemned by both sides), he followed General Whalley's invitation to serve as a chaplain in the parliamentarian army. Army life did not suit him, and his health suffered. Perhaps with his state of health in mind, he returned to his parish in 1647.

The parish of Kidderminster included the market town of the same name and about twenty contiguous villages within twenty miles. In all, the parish consisted of up to four thousand people, or eight hundred families, the vast majority of whom were formally members of the church, but maybe only one per family were serious "professors of religion," Baxter thought. In his view, they were an ignorant, rude, and reveling people, and many in his parish abused alcohol. Even so, for Baxter it was "as honest a town as any I know in England."[12] Its people were not wealthy, most mak-ing their living from weaving. Details concerning the Kidderminster min-istry we will leave for now until discussing *The Reformed Pastor*.

By mid-year 1660, political and ecclesiastical events took unhelpful turns for Richard Baxter. In May, Charles II ascended to the throne. Bax-ter, for a while, was a man in favor, even preaching before the new king on one occasion as a newly appointed chaplain to the monarch. Early success with the royalist party soon turned to frustration; in September, for example, an Act of Parliament restored previously deposed clergy to their livings. One such person was George Dance, one-time vicar of Kid-derminster! Baxter was deposed, much dejected, in spite of a petition, one year later, from sixteen hundred parishioners. Although he was offered the see of Hereford, he did not accept.

For the remaining thirty years of his life, Baxter never again held a reg-ular parish appointment, living privately in or near London. He preached periodically before private groups. In 1662 he married Margaret Charl-ton (d. 1681) whom he loved dearly and who was a loyal companion for many years, sponsoring much of his private preaching. The following years were increasingly given over to writing—"a pen in God's hand." He published some 135 books in his lifetime, followed later with many posthumously published writings. He died on December 8, 1691, and is still generally acknowledged to be the outstanding pastor and teacher of practical Christianity of the Puritan age.

THEMES IN BAXTER'S THEOLOGY

As noted, Baxter shared many theological themes with Puritanism. This brief discussion outlines two positions that identify Baxter's theology in particular insofar as they influence this reading of *The Reformed Pastor*: his avowal of practical Christianity and his idiosyncratic treatment of the doctrine of justification.

Practical Christianity

The Puritans were a people who sought, above all else, to take the Christian faith seriously in every area of their lives. Right belief, disciplined devotion and self-examination, and a passion for reforming action led to an eminently practical form of Christianity. "Puritanism was at heart a spiritual movement, passionately concerned with God and godliness. . . . Puritanism was essentially a movement for church reform, pastoral renewal and evangelism, and spiritual revival."[13]

Richard Baxter fit comfortably into this milieu. Theology, for Baxter, was not a matter of theory or speculation; it was inherently a practical matter, with a practical end in view. As a young man writing in the context of ill health, he noted of his condition that "it caused me to study *Practical Divinity* first, in the most *Practical Books*, in a *Practical Order; doing all purposely for the informing and reforming of my own Soul.*"[14] The theologian James I. Packer sums up Baxter as "perhaps the greatest of Puritan writers on Christian practice."[15]

In 1649 he published his first book, *The Saints' Everlasting Rest*, an 844-page bestseller, written while in the throes of his extraordinarily active ministry at Kidderminster and at a point when he thought he was dying (again!). Central to the book's development is the hope of glory as a strengthening in the midst of trial. Henceforth a stream of books on practical divinity flowed from his pen, covering such a variety of topics as conversion, directions for weak and "out of sorts" Christians, church unity, self-denial, hypocrisy, self-ignorance, the life of faith, the poor man's family, and so on. His practical divinity culminated in the massive 1,143-page tome, *A Christian Directory*, published in 1673, in which he attempted a sum of the theology of the Christian life, "directing Christians how to use their knowledge and faith; how to improve all helps and means, and to perform all duties; how to overcome temptations, and to escape or mortify every sin" (from the subtitle). His argument develops according to the scheme of doctrine, reason, and use. He wrote it partly so that "the younger and more unfurnished and unexperienced sorts of ministers, might have a promptuary at hand, for practical resolutions and directions on the subjects that they have need to deal in."[16]

This practical divinity is seen on virtually every page of *The Reformed Pastor*, beginning with the opening words by which he addressed his audience of ministers.

> See that the work of saving grace be thoroughly wrought in your own souls. Take heed to yourselves, lest you be void of that saving grace of God which you offer to others, and be strangers to the effectual working of that gospel which you preach; and lest, while you proclaim to the world the necessity of a Saviour, your own hearts should neglect him, and you should miss of an interest in him and his saving benefits. Take heed to yourselves, lest you perish, while you call upon others to take heed of perishing; and lest you famish yourselves while you prepare food for them.[17]

Referring to the theme of his preaching, Baxter wrote that, "The thing which I daily opened to them, and with greatest importunity laboured to imprint upon their minds, was the fundamental principles of Christianity."[18] Baxter was above all else, then, what today we would call a practical theologian.

The Doctrine of Justification

Baxter taught a doctrine of justification that contained elements of Roman, Reformed, and Arminian perspectives. His chief concern was to counter the threat of antinomianism, which understood salvation not only to have been accomplished through Christ, but also to have already come, and the proponents of which argued that law-keeping has no place in the economy of salvation. This view saw justification as an act of God in eternity that antedates faith, and faith as but the declaration of what has already occurred for the elect. Baxter, in contrast, argued that if the law's demands have been eternally met, we would have no need to keep the law a second time by our own acts. Faith would become, then, a search for confidence in salvation rather than for conversion.[19] He leaned, then, to the other side of the debate, in the direction of Arminianism, believing that a human component was still present in salvation, adopting a position that came to be known as "Baxterian" or "neonomian." In this position he sought to maintain the priority appropriate to God's grace in Jesus Christ, while insisting on a legitimate place for human responsibility.

Two aspects of Baxter's synthesis of the divine and human elements in the doctrine of justification should be noted: first, his theology of the new covenant and the believer's entrance into it, and second, his understanding of justification as a continuous process.[20] In the first place, while orthodox theology taught that Christ satisfied the demands of God's law in the sinner's place, Baxter taught that Christ satisfied the giver of the law, procuring a change in the demands of the law from legal obedience to faith. Two kinds of righteousness are thus necessary for salvation: the righteousness of Christ, which obtains a new law for us, and the faith of the convert that is imputed also as righteousness. Christ's righteousness is the "meritorious cause," while our faith is the "condition." Asked Baxter, "Are we in any way Justified by our own performed Righteousness? Answer: yes."[21] Faith is then imputed for righteousness in obedience to God's new law.

In the second place, Baxter developed a doctrine of continuous justification in which he tried to incorporate into his thinking the need to ameliorate the judgment to come at the end of the age by a life of faithful covenant-keeping. Here Baxter tried to incorporate the Reformed perspective that faith without works is dead faith, and to argue in so doing that works counted for something in the economy of salvation. "Covenant-making may admit you, but it's Covenant-keeping that must continue you in your priviledges."[22] When provoked to respond to the charge that this was a "Romanizing" of the doctrine of justification, his response was unequivocal: "If this be Justification by Works, I am for it."[23] Baxter's teaching clearly indicated the need for a human part to be conjoined to God's act for one's salvation.

No less a sympathetic modern interpreter than James I. Packer regards Baxter as a brilliant theologian but something of a disaster.[24] Baxter, Packer maintains, cast his theology in the rationalistic language of seventeenth-century political theory; sin is construed in terms of a crime against God, with little sense of its interior and spiritual dimension. Christ is seen as the head of God's government, and his death as a component in salvation but without substitutionary significance. Faith is an act of will and intentionality rather than trust and relationship with God. And God, perhaps ironically, he understands as a lawgiver who changes the law—undercutting, as it were, God's own holiness, opening the door to a permissive view of God, characteristic of later liberalism. With Baxter, natural theology and religious moralism clearly entered into the fold of nonconformist theology. As one commentator tersely put it, referring to Baxter's theology, "It looked as if in the last resort Paul must be saved from himself."[25] As we turn to consider and learn from Baxter's brilliance and success as a pastor and evangelist it is, as Packer notes, sadly fitting that Baxter's church in Kidderminster today is Unitarian![26]

THE REFORMED PASTOR

The book most associated with Richard Baxter, *Gildas Silvianus: or The Reformed Pastor*, grew out of his commitment to speak to the local association of ministers, on the occasion of a day of recollection to be held on December 4, 1655. "Our business here this day," he noted, "is to humble our souls before the Lord for our past negligence, and to implore God's assistance in our work for the time to come."[27] Illness prevented his attendance, but he expanded his offering from an address to a hurriedly written, poorly organized, and rather long book,[28] dedicated "to my reverend and dearly beloved brethren, the faithful ministers of Christ."[29] Reportedly, Baxter sent it to the press without editing or proofreading the text,[30] and it is prolix and repetitive. Nevertheless, as the historian Hugh Martin correctly notes, "Behind it lay the authority of his work in Kidderminster. There are many books for ministers about their work, but there is probably none more searching, impressive, persuasive and helpful than this. It should be read by every minister."[31] Its value, at least for pastors today, lies in Baxter's capacity to lay out a vision for ministry that remains a challenge because of its urgency and clear sense of purpose regarding God's claim upon people's lives. *The Reformed Pastor* is the most important book on ministry to come from the Puritan period, and arguably from the pen of an Englishman of any age. Baxter, it can well be argued, was incomparable as a pastor and evangelist.

A few words on the title: the reformed pastor, as noted earlier, is not the Calvinist or Presbyterian pastor, but the quickened or renewed pastor, one who, in the words of the guiding text, keeps watch over himself or herself, and over all the flock, of which the Holy Spirit has made one a pastor, to shepherd the church of God that he obtained with the blood of his Son (Acts 20:28). Transformed ministry comes from transformed pastors. The odd title, *Gildas Silvianus*, is after two early Christian writers who were notable for their ability to speak freely to the pastors of the churches. Says Baxter in plain words: "If God would but reform the ministry, and set them on their duties zealously and faithfully, the people would certainly be reformed. All churches either rise or fall as the ministry doth rise or fall (not in riches or worldly grandeur), but in knowledge, zeal and ability for their work."[32]

The book was written for ministers in the context of their need for confession of sin because of their dual failure to attend to their own spiritual state and to catechize and instruct their people adequately. Baxter's tone is schoolmasterish and moralistic—"I know myself to be unworthy to be your monitor; but a monitor you must have"[33]—but his intent is the honest reformation of the practice of their ministry, according to Baxter's Kidderminster pattern, which we will address presently. He writes as one burdened by a message for his clerical brothers: "Oh, if we did but study half as much to affect and amend our own hearts, as we do those of our hearers, it would not be with many of us as it is!"[34] That goal sets the preachy tone, and although Baxter himself is apologetic for it, his nature was to write in such a manner. Yet he pursues his goal with a self-revealing honesty that is remarkable and often disarming. His passion for and understanding of the pastoral task, his keen theological mind—in spite of critical questions arising from his theology—and his sharp-edged analysis of the dangers that ministers face make this an accessible and enduring contribution to the classical tradition in pastoral theology.

Baxter wrote on three important areas: (1) the need for the pastor to attend to his or her relationship with God; (2) conversion as a dominant pastoral goal; and (3) taking heed to all the flock as Baxter's controlling pastoral metaphor.

Take Heed to Yourselves

While Baxter's practice of ministry tends to capture the attention of the textbooks, he begins his book with, and returns recurrently throughout the book to, the spiritual formation of the pastor, as have many of the authors we have studied thus far. In fact, as a matter of priority he is more concerned with the pastor's life in God than with the parishioner's, because adequate attention to the latter is possible only by one who has paid attention to the former. Baxter's approach was not a matter of pastoral technique, skillfully applied; *The Reformed Pastor* is not really a textbook on pastoral care. Rather, his approach was to apply a spiritual and theological understanding of human beings to the work of the pastoral ministry, which begins with the continuing conversion of the pastor and leads to the conversion of the parishioner. Faithful ministry is the consequence, then, of a reformed or spiritually renewed pastor. "If it not be your daily business to study your own hearts, and to subdue corruption, and to walk with God—if you make not this a work to which you constantly attend, all will go wrong, and you will starve your hearers."[35] Baxter's unambiguous conviction concerning the conversion and spiritual renewal of the pastor can hardly be overemphasized, for that emphasis is rarely found today in much pastoral theology literature. Today the focus is more likely to fall on the pastor's mental health.

In the opening section of the book, Baxter calls for pastoral integrity that reflects congruence between a pastor's inner disposition and relationship with God, on the one hand, and his or her outward ministry, on the other. "See that the work of saving grace be thoroughly wrought in your own souls,"[36] he counsels. "O sirs, how many men have preached Christ, and yet have perished for want of a saving interest in him!"[37] Baxter insists that the pastor can hardly minister a grace that he or she does not know firsthand. An unregenerate pastor leads worship to an unknown God, preaches an unknown Christ, and prays through an unknown Spirit. The dominant concern for evangelism begins at home!

Further, the pastor should not rest content with being in a state of grace, but must attend to relationship with God day by day. Why? Because "that which is most on your hearts, is like to be most in their ears."[38] Without constant attention to God and consistent spiritual vigilance, ministry will fall apart. "For your people's sakes, therefore, look to your hearts."[39] To this end, a pastor must be frequent in prayer and meditation. When a pastor pays attention to the work of grace within his or her own life and faith, that same work of grace may appear in the sermons that the pastor preaches. To preach a word that is not from the heart is to allow example (even if hidden) to contradict doctrine, and so to lay a stumbling block before the blind, which may be to the congregation's spiritual ruin. Beware, then, says Baxter, "lest you unsay with your lives, what you say with your tongues."[40] And again: "O sirs, all your preaching and persuading of others, will be but dreaming and vile hypocrisy, till the work be thoroughly done upon your own hearts."[41] The point is that the pastor who is privately unfaithful to God through the neglect of his or her own life in God is not to be trusted with the care of other people's souls.

Baxter drives home his point by drawing attention to what most surely was a problem then, as today: the failure of clergy to live lives appropriate to their calling. The consequence of failure is a scattering of the flock of Christ: "Take heed to yourselves, because there are many eyes upon you, and there are many to observe your falls. . . . If other men may sin without observation, so cannot you."[42] Baxter understood that clergy are public figures whose failures—scandal, carelessness in attention to duties, and hypocrisy—can do terrible harm to a congregation.

According to Baxter certain professional sins are especially dangerous for pastors: "Brethren, may I expostulate this case a little with my own heart and yours, that we may see the evil of our sin, and be reformed!"[43]

First, somewhat traditionally, is the sin of pride, corresponding to which is humility. Baxter writes that, "A proud preacher of humility is at least a self-condemning man," and "Woe to him to who takes up the fame of godliness instead of godliness!"[44] Baxter urges pastors to be students of humility because "humility is not a mere ornament of a Christian, but an essential part of the new creature."[45] The second sin, he notes, is negligence to duties of study, and to appropriate vigor and liveliness in preaching and teaching. "Alas! How imperfectly and how negligently do the most, even of those that we take to be godly ministers, go through their work!"[46] He is especially harsh in criticism of dull preachers.

> A sleepy preacher will hardly awaken drowsy sinners. . . . Speak to your people as to men that must be awakened . . . and to make not only the matter that is preached, but also the manner of preaching instrumental to the work.[47]

Third, he cautions against being overly attracted to worldly gains. Like John Chrysostom before him, he counsels a wariness of praise, noting that the lack of wariness is "an epidemical malady."[48] Similarly, he counsels against the temporizing of the gospel ministry for love of money, especially when the minister's financial gain results in less pastoral help.

Fourth, he mentions the lack of concern among ministers for the peace and unity of the church, and the adoption instead of a factional attitude. Baxter pleads for moderation to replace what he calls new-dividing zeal.

Finally, in the tradition of Martin Bucer, he warns against the failure to exercise church discipline in response to sinners reluctant to repent and amend their lives. Pastors, he notes, are reluctant to engage in converse with sinful people about their sin for fear that the work is troublesome and painful.

As a pastor Baxter understood that the pastor's personal faith and moral behavior, private and public, were every bit as important as the content of the sermon when it came to the point of affecting the congregation's receiving the gospel. Much has changed since Baxter's day, but not the connivance and duplicity of the human heart, nor the seductions to which ministers are especially exposed. Arguably, the pitfalls are more numerous today, for we live in a morally permissive society in which Christian virtue is largely expelled from public life. By beginning his book with these arguments, Baxter emphasized two areas of pastoral theological instruction and practice that still today receive scant attention: spiritual formation and moral education. What does it mean, spiritually, theologically, and morally, that saving grace is to be thoroughly wrought in a pastor's life? Ministers, seminaries, and denominations must struggle with other important issues in their concern for a faithful ministry, but no other issue is more important than the sanctification of the pastor.

The modern pastoral care movement has rightly and helpfully stressed the benefit of psychological maturity and mental health. Increasingly, too, we have seen the rise of appropriate concerns for both professional ministerial ethics and the understanding of role boundaries and responsibilities. We have moved part of the way in the right direction. But the concerns for the pastor's spiritual and moral formation remain largely unaddressed. To be healthy and whole is not enough; holiness and obedient discipleship are also expected of a pastor. A pastor's and the church's attention both to the integrity of spiritual and moral life, and to the need to grow and mature into an ever richer and more converted life in God, remain necessary conditions for faithful ministry. The point is, says Baxter, speaking to pastors, that "the enemy hath a special eye upon you."[49] To ministers, then and now, his admonition is, "Take heed to yourselves, for you have a depraved nature, and sinful inclinations, as well as others."[50] To give this topic the highest attention is to follow the lead of Richard Baxter.

Conversion: Baxter's Dominant Pastoral Goal

Whatever else we can learn from Baxter's approach to pastoral care, of singular importance in his own life and ministry was a concern for the plight of the unconverted.

> O remember, when you are talking with the unconverted, that now you have an opportunity to save a soul, and to rejoice the angels of heaven, and to rejoice Christ himself, to cast Satan out of a sinner, and to increase the family of God![51]

Baxter's concern for the salvation of the people of his parish is woven through the tapestry of *The Reformed Pastor*. Clearly in view always is the person standing before the judgment seat of God, no matter their state of grace. The concern for pastoral care as evangelism is a recurring chorus being sung, sometimes on front stage, at other times in the background.

Writing in the Dedication to his colleagues in ministry, Baxter sums up his overriding passion: "It is the mere necessity of the souls of men, and my desire of their salvation, and of the prosperity of the Church, which forceth me to this arrogance and immodesty (of writing the book), if it so must be called."[52] The concern for people's salvation is not to exclude other important pastoral tasks, of course, for he explicitly insists on the need for guiding and building up the flock, caring for families and the sick, private admonishment, and public discipline. But the priority is clearly set upon evangelism. Thus, the great task, within and through all pastoral work, "is to be the guide of sinners to heaven."[53] "Ministerial work must be carried on purely for God and the salvation of souls."[54] Failure to attend to this priority has unspeakable consequences for the parishioner and the pastor, he warns. "We must labour, in a special manner for the conversion of the unconverted. The work of conversion is the first and great thing we must drive at; after this we must labour with all our might."[55] In view of this imperative, Baxter confessed that frequently he was "forced to neglect that which should tend to the further increase of knowledge in the godly, because of the lamentable necessity of the unconverted."[56]

Ministerial work, including evangelism, Baxter wrote, must be carried on diligently and laboriously, prudently and orderly, with plainness and simplicity, with humility, mixing as appropriate severity and mildness, seriousness, earnestness and zeal, always with tender love for God's people, exercising patience and reverence, with pious regard for the expectation of success, all the while knowing our own insufficiency and depending only on Christ and the fellowship of colleagues in ministry. Further, "Satan will not be charmed out of his possession: we must lay siege to the souls of sinners, which are his garrison, and find out where his chief strength lieth, and lay the battery of God's ordnance against it, and ply it close, til a breach is made; and then suffer them not by their shifts to repair it again."[57] His military metaphor suggests that pastoral work as evangelism is warfare against an implacable and untiring enemy that takes all of the spiritual and moral strength and energy available to the pastor. In view of this, the opening emphasis on the spiritual fitness of the pastor is clearly appropriate.

What did Baxter understand by evangelism? As did the Puritans in general, he likened people to spiders suspended above a roaring fire. They were "within a step of hell."[58] Their plight was desperate. Baxter believed that souls not won to Christ would perish. Pastoral care is care for the person who must eventually stand before God, the Judge. Because of this, Baxter tolerated no cotton-mouthed approach to sin and salvation. Care, he argued, is not merely to bring succor if a person's eternal status is in doubt. Baxter adopted a conditional covenant view of Christ's death as a universal redemption that was penal and vicarious, but not substitutionary, "in virtue of which God has made a new law offering pardon and amnesty to the penitent. Repentance and faith, being obedience to this law, are the believer's personal saving righteousness."[59] According to

Baxter, the work of conversion consists of two parts: "First, the informing of the judgment in the essential principles of religion; Second, The change of the will by the efficacy of the truth."[60]

For Baxter, the covenant of grace contained and communicated God's promises—but conditionally.[61] Thus, in *Practical Works* he wrote:

> The terms or conditions which God requireth of man in his covenant are, consent, fidelity or performance. . . . He consenteth to be actually our God when we consent to be his people . . . but the sincere performance of the duties of the relation which we consent to, are needful afterwards to continue the relation.[62]

This "neo-nomianism" or "new law" has doubtful theological virtue, not least because it is in the end staggeringly unevangelical in its casting of persons back upon their own faith and obedience, rather than upon Christ. Is Christ our justification, or are faith and obedience our justification? Also in the light of his doctrine of the atonement, a certain earnest moralism arises in Baxter's tone and content. Baxter has in his attitude and sense of need for moral effort a Pelagian spirit, both in the way in which he pushes himself to the limit, and in what he demands of others. The obvious point is that to rely on the fulfillment of conditions is ultimately to rely upon one's own works.

In spite of the serious theological deficiencies in his understanding of the atonement and justification, however, Baxter did nevertheless understand that pastoral care is care for the person who must stand before God. This ultimate framework prescribes all of ministry. The challenge Baxter leaves for pastoral work today in this regard is to develop an evangelistic pastoral care; but this care, we must insist, is evangelical as God's good news to the sinner as grace rather than as law, while taking seriously the call to faith, repentance, and discipleship. Baxter reminds us that trying to bring comfort in the midst of life's tragedies but failing to address a person's life in and before God is no care at all. The theological development of pastoral care to be understood and practiced in terms of soteriology and eschatology continues to be Baxter's legacy, and one that places him in the tradition of classical pastoral theology. We have seen this theme in all of the texts studied to date, but it is especially evident in the two Protestant pastors, Bucer and Baxter. Clearly the legacy of pastoral care in the classic tradition is the recovery of pastoral evangelism as a significant priority for pastoral work that is faithful to the inherent nature of the gospel as a gospel of God's redemption. This approach necessitates a return to a clear christological and soteriological foundation for pastoral theology, without which evangelism has no basis.

Take Heed to All the Flock:
Individualized Pastoral Care

We come now to the aspect of Baxter's pastoral care that is probably best known, namely, to consider pastoral care as a personal ministry to persons. The exercise of this charge is perhaps Baxter's greatest genius as a pastor.

Acts 20:28, Baxter's controlling text, bids pastors to attend to all the flock. The pastor must know and have concern for everyone in his or her charge.[63] The details of Baxter's agenda for pastoral care reflect the goal. Not only must every church have a pastor, who is in effect the bishop of the congregation, but the size of the congregation must be appropriate to enable personal knowledge of each parishioner. "Flocks must ordinarily be no greater than we are capable of overseeing. . . . If the pastoral office consists in overseeing all the flock, then surely the number of souls under the care of each pastor must not be greater than he is able to take such heed to as is here required."[64] If necessary, Baxter thinks, a pastor should, out of his own pocket, pay for an assistant in order to ensure that adequate pastoral care is given to the people. Merely preaching well is not enough. "Will preaching a good sermon serve the turn, while you never look more after them, but deny them that closer help that is necessary, and alienate that maintenance to your own flesh, which should provide relief for so many souls?"[65]

Theologically, as well, Baxter takes his lead from Acts 20:28: "Keep watch over yourselves and over all the flock, of which the Holy Spirit has made you overseers, to shepherd the church of God that he obtained with the blood of his own Son." First, the pastor, as overseer of the flock, is bishop to his or her people. "Bishop" is not a title or position of honor. As bishop, a pastor guides the people to heaven. Everything must be done to be worthy of this office. Ministers must be diligent students, constant at prayer, and hard at work. Second, the call is from the Holy Spirit, sent from heaven. Baxter understands the need for institutional process, but the primary ordination is charismatic rather than episcopal. Third, "it is the *Church* of GOD which we must oversee—that Church for which the world is chiefly upheld, which is sanctified by the Holy Ghost, which is the mystical body of Christ, that Church with which angels are present. . . . Oh what a charge it is that we have undertaken!"[66] Fourth, he admonishes pastors, "every time we look upon our congregations, let us believingly remember that they are the purchase of Christ's blood, and therefore should be regarded by us with the deepest interest and the most tender affection. Oh, think what a confusion it will be to a negligent minister, at the last day, to have the blood of the Son of God pleaded against him; and for Christ to say, 'It was the purchase of my blood of which thou didst make so light, and dost thou think to be saved by it thyself?'"[67] Here, and in common with the classical tradition, Baxter appreciates that the special and glorious charge given to pastors carries a terrible accountability.

The issues Baxter raised are worth reiteration: not only must the pastor know his or her flock, but the flock must be of a size that does not overwhelm the possibility of individualized pastoral care. Further, the ministry must be such that it includes priority given to pastoral care; good preaching and the careful administration of the parish program are not adequate. Finally, the ministry must be understood in terms of the extraordinary nature of the call from God and the responsibility placed thereby on the minister. Pastoral ministry is truly a high calling, to be discharged with utmost seriousness.

We come now to the work for which Baxter is most famous, which marked his ministry at Kidderminster as exemplary, and which was the basis for its success. In Baxter's own words:

> I set two Days a Week apart, for this Employment: my (faithful unwearied) Assistant and myself, took fourteen Families every Week; those in the Town came to us in our Houses . . . ; those in the Parish my Assistant went to, to their Houses: First they recited the Catechism to us (a Family only being present at a time, and no Stranger admitted); after that I first helpt them to understand it, and next enquired modestly into the State of their Souls, and lastly, endeavoured to set all home to the convincing, awakening and resolving of their Hearts according to their several Conditions; bestowing about an Hour (and the Labour of a Sermon) with every Family. [And] though the first time they came with Fear and Backwardness, after that they longed for their turn to come again. Few Families went from me without some tears, or seemingly serious promises for a Godly life. . . . If any of them were stalled through Ignorance or Bashfulness, I forbore to press them any further to Answers, but made them Hearers, and either examined others, or turned all into Instruction and Exhortation. . . . All the Afternoons on Mondays and Tuesdays, I spent in this: [and] my Assistant spent the Mornings of the same Days in the same Employment.[68]

In all, Baxter and his assistant personally visited with the whole congregation, about eight hundred families, perhaps four thousand people, once a year in this manner. Even so, "how small a matter is it to speak to a man only once a year. . . . Yet we are in hope of some fruit."[69]

The center of this extraordinary round of pastoral care was the work of catechesis, teaching the Christian faith. Even as a pastor, he remained something of a schoolmaster, not only instructing his people, but also giving away his books for them to read. He was truly a teaching elder. Little do the parishioners know, he argued, "that the minister is in the church, as the schoolmaster is in his school, to teach and take an account of everyone in particular; and that all Christians, ordinarily, must be disciples or scholars in some such school."[70] He acted on the view that grace enters into our lives by growth in understanding. Although his approach is heavily didactic, something profoundly right surely exists in wishing for his people an ever-deepening understanding of Christian faith.

Not surprisingly, so thorough and focused a pastoral ministry met with success among the people: "I find more outward signs of success with most that do come, than from all my public preaching to them."[71] If this judgment is even remotely accurate, it speaks volumes for the evangelical power of personal pastoral instruction and care for *all* the people of God. His discipline was not harsh, but with experience more sympathetic, though it did arouse opposition (one time he was caricatured in effigy at the annual town fair). Also, his parishioners were invited to receive his ministry: "we could be Pastors to none against their wills."[72] "I cannot say yet that one family hath refused to come to me, and but few persons excused themselves."[73] Nevertheless, a pastoral discipline was also applied that through instruction called people to repentance and renewal of life. The net result was that the church was crowded on Sunday morning, and an enlargement had to be built to expand the seating to about one thousand.[74] New life came to the congregation. Many were converted. Family worship became a habit.

> When I came thither first there was about one family in a street that worshipped God and called on his name, and when I came away there were some streets where there was not passed one family in the side of a street that did not so, and that did not, by professing serious godliness, give us hopes of their sincerity. And those families which were the worst, being inns and alehouses, usually *some persons* in each house did seem to be religious.[75]

While mainline Protestants today often respond unfavorably to Puritan writers, *The Reformed Pastor* continues to be read with salutary appreciation by pastors who wish to redress the ambiguities that arise in theology and ministry. The reasons are not difficult to discover. Pastoral work today proceeds largely through acts of kindness, support, and encouragement. Specialists in the field tend to be skilled in psychology and counseling. What is missing is the one thing most to be commended in *The Reformed Pastor*, namely, a sense of seriousness about a person's situation outside of relationship with Jesus Christ. Is it no coincidence today that confusion over Christology in the mainline churches of North America and Europe and the loss of direction in pastoral care seem to be features of Protestant Christianity? Baxter writes with such clarity and conviction about the Gospel, the person of the pastor, and the essential tasks of pastoral work that he is received as bringing a fresh and challenging perspective to a confused and dispirited profession. He quickens his readers with urgency about and the necessity for the pastor's work, and reawakens the perspective, now long dormant, of the minister as the teaching elder charged with the Christian instruction of the people. In spite of difficulties with Baxter's theological position and his long-winded writing style, *The Reformed Pastor* remains a great work on the pastoral ministry that not only stands within the classical tradition of pastoral theology, but that lends support to the argument that this tradition continues to be a source of fruitful provocation for our thinking about pastoral work today.

Conclusion: Pastoral Theology in the Classical Tradition

Tend the flock of God that is in your charge, exercising the oversight, not under compulsion but willingly, as God would have you do it—not for sordid gain but eagerly. Do not lord it over those in your charge, but be examples to the flock. And when the chief shepherd appears, you will win the crown of glory that never fades away.

1 Peter 5:2–4

Now the task is to identify the contemporary shape of pastoral theology in the classical tradition, drawing upon what has gone before in order to suggest a trajectory into the future. In what follows I offer a brief, but I hope provocative, sketch of a pastoral theology and an understanding of the practice of pastoral care that are open to learning from the pastors of the past whom we have studied. This essay is merely a "preface to pastoral theology," offered as theses and themes for exploration.

As noted in the Introduction to this book, the goal in reading ancient texts in pastoral theology is not for us to "do pastoral care" in a way similar to pastors from other ages. The goal, rather, is to allow these classical texts to provoke us into critical thinking by disturbing our calm, culture-bound assumptions concerning ministry, and in so doing to suggest avenues for exploration. As each text has been discussed, I have identified issues that arise for pastoral work today. Now we must pull all of that together to suggest in an ordered way the thinking about and the practice of ministry today, informed directly by a reading of these ancient authors.

Arising out of a reading of classical texts in pastoral theology I offer eight points for reflection.

Pastoral Theology and Pastoral Care Are Explicitly Confessional in Content

In a core or foundational way, pastoral work is not based on anything other than Jesus Christ clothed with his gospel given as and under the marks of Word and sacraments. As such, pastoral work is a discipline of the church and is distinguished in this way from other helping acts, even when administered by Christians. The classical tradition insists on congruence between doctrine and care, between pulpit and counseling room. As I have pointed out, this approach is in striking contrast to much pastoral theological literature and pastoral practice today, which casts pastoral work largely in terms of the social sciences, and with only a loose sense of Christian faith giving it form and content. The classical pastoral writers, whatever other strengths and weaknesses may be identified with them, were clear and firm in their sense of the closest possible connection between the faith of the church given in the primary doctrines and the practice of ministry. In particular, classical pastoral theology is strongly cast in a christological, soteriological, and eschatological framework. Pastoral care, in this case, is understood and practiced with a deep and abiding sense of confessional theological identity and clarity with regard to the central tenets of Christian faith.

Pastoral theology today that seeks to build on the classical tradition will be written and practiced as the practical theology of the acting God whose nature and purpose are revealed uniquely and savingly in and through Jesus Christ for the salvation of all who by grace believe and trust in him. A specifically Christian pastoral theology in the classic tradition, then, will be a pastoral theology of the incarnation and the atonement, and of the primary doctrines that follow. As such, this pastoral theology will be both evangelical (in the sense of being centered in Jesus Christ) and evangelistic (in the sense of being primarily concerned with people in their lives before God through faith in Jesus Christ).

Pastoral Theology Is a Discipline, and Pastoral Care Is a Practice, Deeply Rooted at All Points in the Study of the Bible

Again in contrast to the pastoral literature of today, the classical authors were so saturated in scripture that their writing and practice are, in effect, lived biblical theology. Now we can rightly challenge their hermeneutics and the conclusions that their Bible studies produced, for they remain always the people of their own ages. What we surely cannot challenge is their very serious intention to allow their thinking about and their practice of ministry to be developed from and controlled by their reading and study of scripture.

Undoubtedly much information about pastoral counseling has been learned in recent times from the study of "living human documents." There is now no going back from that. Pastoral theology will always be a discipline in close conversation with psychology. Pastors, after all, have to deal with people. The classical authors are each, in their own ways, practicing psychologists who have amazing insights into the human condition and the workings of the human mind. But pastoral theologians and pastors in the classical tradition will engage in this conversation with psychology on the basis of their own study of scripture and the Christian doctrinal tradition. A contemporary pastoral theology and practice in the classical tradition will be notable as a biblical pastoral theology and practice first of all, in which room is again available for exegesis and careful theological construction on this basis.

Ministry Is a High Calling to a Holy Office, the Faithful Exercise of Which Is Necessary for the Salvation of Christ's People

The faithful discharge of pastoral work is a godly charge given to the few called by God's providence to that office, whose work is necessary for the life and ministry of the church. The classical authors have no diffidence at all over the divine ordering, the given authority, and the corresponding responsibility of the pastoral office. They see it as a vital part of God's gracious dispensation given through the church for the salvation of the world. A contemporary pastoral theology in the classical tradition sets the understanding and practice of ministry in the context of soteriology and eschatology. This outlook is in stark contrast to the declining sense of worth in which pastoral work today is held in society in general (and even, one suspects, in the church!), and which social perspective no doubt disables pastors in the faithful exercise of their duties.

Pastors are men and women who are called, educated, installed, and empowered to announce God's forgiveness, declare God's healing, proclaim God's word, celebrate God's sacramental presence, call forth and guide the living of the amended life, teach the truth of the Christian faith, and, in ministries of compassion, live in community with the people in their pastoral charge. Outside of their work, the church could not exist. For this reason, pastors are ordained to the ministry of the Word and sacraments—to the ministry of what the Reformed tradition has often called the ordinary means of grace by and through which God builds and blesses the church unto eternal salvation. The classical tradition would have the ministers of today attend to these tasks and dwell often upon the magnitude of their responsibility.

Pastoral Work Demands Taking Heed to Oneself to the End That He or She Is Theologically, Spiritually, and Ethically a Mature Person

The classical pastoral theologians were men from ages other than our own who advocated and adopted spiritual and ascetical practices that are no longer typical. The two Gregorys, Chrysostom, and Baxter, for example, were chronically sick men due in part to their own mortifications and overwork. Ignoring their frailties and oddities, what makes them emulatable? What truth, amid their excesses, can we uphold? While we may not follow them in the particular styles in which they prepared themselves for service and lived out their obedience to God, their lesson remains: pastors today are also called to a disciplined life before God. The reason is as true now as it was in the times of our authors: ministry is not "natural" work in the sense that it is within our human compass and possibility. It is, in a sense, an alien work that demands great transformation by God, for the want of which the work of the pastor cannot succeed. In fact, the lack of interior renewal will lead to an outward ministry that will likely destroy both the pastor and his or her congregation.

An abiding theme in the classical tradition is expressed in Baxter's axiom: "Take heed to yourself." Each author in his own way writes about its necessity. This appeal is not, however, to self-fulfillment, but to disciplined attention to one's life in God. The classical authors understood that unless a pastor is within a deepening process of conversion and sanctification, that pastor is in grave danger of both self-deceit and building ministry upon the loose foundation of his or her own unexamined needs. Only on the secure ground of ever becoming a renewed pastor through an examined life in God is he or she able henceforth to take heed with safety to the flock given into his or her care. Pastors, then, are called to live examined lives of theological, spiritual, and ethical maturity.

God Will Hold Pastors Accountable for the Exercise of the Pastoral Office and the Care of God's People

Pastoral accountability surely is one of the great surprises found in the classical texts, and perhaps the most fearful. Each author, often in thundering prose, not only denounces faithless pastors, but warns with no uncertainty that God will hold pastors accountable for the loss of people given into their pastoral charge. When seen from a soteriological and eschatological perspective, failure in pastoral work is terrible indeed. This accountability is a corollary to the high calling of the office, indicative of the importance of pastoral work in the scheme of God's eternity.

What form should this accountability take in practice? Clearly all who seek pastoral office need to be made explicitly aware of the danger to themselves should they accept the call inadvertently or enter into the practice of ministry carelessly. Strong and informed spiritual counsel must surely be made available to ordinands, for about this issue today widespread ignorance abounds within the church and among the clergy. Further, seminar-

ies and candidacy processes have an institutional responsibility both to prepare candidates for ministry so that they are theological, spiritually, ethi-
cally, and professionally fit for office and to equip them to discern the
nature of their responsibilities and what these demand personally from and
of the pastor. In other words, the classical tradition in pastoral theology
would teach that the highest spiritual priority is to be given to in-depth discernment regarding the call to ministry and the identification of the appropriate gifts of grace, with encouragement to resist until one is convinced
that acceptance of call is the demand of obedience to God. For the sake of
candidates and the congregations they will prospectively serve, preparation
for ordination should be a very difficult, intrusive, and demanding process.

Pastoral Care Is the Art of Arts

We live in a time of burgeoning skills for ministry, which is entirely to be
welcomed. But the classical tradition also imposes a caveat: Do not reduce
ministry to the exercise of skills, to pastoral techniques. For a certain
dimension of ministry, while to be learned, is much more than a skill. The
vague phrase, "the art of arts," is difficult to define. It suggests that pastoral work is an aesthetic discipline, one that requires a certain cast of
mind, an intuitive apprehension that is deeply guided by the things of God
and an understanding of the nature of people. The discipline is not without skills, of course, but it is more than skills. Pastoral work, we might suggest, is given its shape by a spiritual apperception that is profoundly
controlled by a conceptual grasp of Christian doctrine. As such, pastoral
work is a calling that is best learned through apprenticeship to a master
pastor (the Orthodox have the wonderful concept of an arch-priest or
proto-presbyter), and by critical reflection on ministry, a process, one
fears, that largely ends when a student graduates from seminary.

Faithful pastoral work is the fruit of wisdom. In the first place, pastoral
wisdom means a knowledge of Jesus Christ, who is the wisdom of God
(1 Cor. 1:30). In the second place, pastoral wisdom involves a willingness
to learn "on the job." In the third place, pastoral wisdom involves a willingness to listen to the accumulated knowledge of the great pastors of the
Christian tradition. The loss of this historical knowledge especially is a
blight on the practice of ministry today that has very serious consequences.

Pastoral Ministry Is Contextual and Situational

Each of the classical writers dwelt at length on the complexities of pastoral
work. Person and circumstance must shape the pastoral response. What

is helpful for one may be hurtful for another. A pastoral response that is correct at one time may be inappropriate at another. A pastor must thus develop a discerning wisdom in order to know what remedy to apply in each case. Pastoral work is not formulaic.

This statement has two implications. First, and by necessity, pastoral work is reflective and prayerful. The work is not hurried, but is rather done by pastors who have time and take time. No doubt this notion calls into question approaches to ministry today that have become largely administrative and programmatic, leaving less time for the kind of attentive care that the classical tradition advises. Second, pastors must ever grow in their knowledge and understanding of people. They must be psychologists in the deepest sense, becoming men and women who understand the souls of their people and who know how to identify and treat soul-sickness. This task involves a profound knowledge of the ways of God and of the wiles of human avoidance.

Pastors Deeply Committed to the Church Wrote the Classical Texts

As pastoral theology has become an academic discipline with its own academic guild and criteria for advancement, writing in the field tends to be by university-trained and academically appointed scholars, who may or may not have served a congregation as pastor. The classical tradition makes a case for pastoral work to be primarily accountable to the gospel and the church in the context of the gap that undoubtedly exists today between the academy and the congregation. However that gap is characterized and experienced, pastors should receive with due critical awareness, and pastoral theologians should offer with appropriate humility, the fruit of academic research and writing. Perhaps, too, the church should firmly encourage reflective pastors with appropriate education to contribute to the literature on pastoral work, recognizing that their perspective is a valuable contribution also to pastoral theology.

We note also that the authors of the classical texts in pastoral theology were not pastoral theologians as such, but men who were pastors first of all, who secondarily produced works of theology and devotion, some of which concerned pastoral work directly. All lived and wrote beyond the limits of pastoral theology, seeing themselves and their work as part of a larger theological task. This fact calls into question the various specializations that exists in the theological academy today. In the light of the classical tradition in pastoral theology one wonders if, in fact, a discipline called "pastoral theology" really should exist, as if it has some appropriate, distinct identity apart from theological and pastoral work! If pastoral theology has any legitimate identity, it is the identity of a discipline that serves to pull all of the other branches of theological study into the center, to the place where ministry must happen in care for God's people. As such, pastoral theology has the special virtue and grace of being a generalist discipline conducted by especially gifted Christians who know enough to find their way among the other branches of theological inquiry, and who have the godly courage to pull them all together, like the hub holding the spokes of a wheel to the center, in the service of the ministry of the church.

Epilogue: An Ordination
Sermon on 2 Corinthians 11:2

"The Father of the Bride"

God will not be mocked by faithless or incompetent pastors. The importance, and the terror, too, of the pastoral office is no less than that God holds pastors accountable for the spiritual life and indeed the salvation of the people in their charge. This harsh verdict of the great tradition of pastoral theology is found throughout the history of the Church. This tradition, however, is largely unknown in the modern, Western Church, much to the peril of both pastors and people.

St. Gregory of Nazianzus, the great pastoral theologian of the fourth century, cited Ezekiel 3:18 in this regard: "If I say to the wicked, 'You shall surely die,' and you give them no warning, or speak to warn the wicked from their wicked way, in order to save their life, those wicked persons shall die for their iniquity; but their blood I will require at your hand." Note these words from Ezekiel: "their blood I will require at your hand." Gregory responded to the magnitude of the pastoral responsibility and the judgment of God upon those pastors who are not faithful with the refrain: Who is able? Who is able? Who is able? Little wonder, then, that he ran away from ministry immediately upon being ordained, only later to return as an act of obedience. Gregory, you see, understood the grave responsibilities of the pastoral office and the judgment of God upon him were he to exercise that office unfaithfully.

A generation later, St. John Chrysostom, the greatest preacher of the Greek Church, cited Hebrews 13:17: "Obey your leaders and submit to them, for they are keeping watch over your souls and will give an account." There it is again: "and will give an account." Once more the same theme is lifted up from the scriptures: The pastors will be held accountable by God for the spiritual well-being of the people in their charge. If the pastor does not keep watch over the people, the pastor will have to give an explanation to God for failure. John Chrysostom commented that "the fear of this threat continually disturbs my spirit" (*On the Priesthood*, 136).

During Reformation times, Martin Bucer of Strasbourg, the Reformer who wrote that period's most important treatise on pastoral theology, picked up the same theme. Ministers, he wrote, who fail in the evangelical task of bringing their people to Christ will be held accountable for the failure. Bucer follows the great pastors of the past when he understands that the blood of the lambs not brought to Christ will be required of those whom Christ has appointed in his church to be pastors of his flock, to seek their salvation and call them to repentance through the proclamation of the grace of Christ. The Reformer has Ezekiel 34:4 in mind: "You have not strengthened the weak, you have not healed the sick, you have not bound up the injured, you have not brought back the strayed, you have not sought the lost."

Ordaining or installing someone into the pastoral office is very serious business. Yet how often these services are sentimental and trite affairs. We forget that the minister's own salvation may be at stake in his or her faithful fulfillment of the pastoral office. Consider the familiar warning from James 3.1: "Not many of you should become teachers, my brothers and sisters, for you know that we who teach will be judged with greater strictness." To cite St. John Chrysostom again, "What will be the fate and what the punishment of those who ruin, not just one or two or three, but great multitudes? They cannot even plead inexperience, or take refuge in a plea of ignorance or make force and constraint their excuse" (*On the Priesthood*, 136).

Lying behind all of these warnings, of course, is an extremely high view of the call to the pastoral office. The job is not like any other, but a calling from the Most High and Holy God through our Lord Jesus Christ to serve as a minister of the Gospel. The calling is not just a career launched upon, but a life to be given over as an ambassador for God. Always the gravest danger is that people who are called to the pastoral office want to be like everyone else. How easily we trivialize that which is holy and reduce to entertainment that which is most sacred. Too often also the church wants her ministers to be like everyone else. A false democracy of opinion and a deconstruction of ministerial and pastoral authority run amok in the church. This time in the history of the church is very serious, a time that makes extraordinary demands upon the theological acuity, spiritual maturity, and moral honesty of pastors. But, thus it was always so!

Paul has given us a powerful image of the role of the pastor in 2 Corinthians 11:2. To the congregation that he founded at Corinth, he wrote, "I feel a divine jealousy for you, for I promised you in marriage to one husband, to present you as a chaste virgin to Christ." Here Paul portrays himself as the father of the bride, the father of the Christian congregation at Corinth. He is their spiritual father, because he first preached the Gospel to them. "Indeed, in Christ Jesus I became your father through the gospel," he wrote (1 Cor. 4:15). So now he can speak as the father of the bride, asserting his commitment to "marry" his daughter church at Corinth to Christ her Lord. "I promised you in marriage to one husband," he writes. Now is the time of engagement. Paul also looks ahead to the time yet to come when the marriage between Christ and his little community at Corinth will be consummated, as it is presented by Paul as a chaste virgin to the Lord. (See "Conquest, Control and the Cross," Brian K. Peterson, *Interpretation*, July 1998.)

Paul goes on to express his fear, however, that his "daughter," the church at Corinth, may be seduced before the wedding day. "I am afraid that as the serpent deceived Eve by its cunning, your thoughts will be led astray from a sincere and pure devotion to Christ" (2 Cor. 11:3). Who will seduce his "daughter?" Of whom and of what is he afraid? He is afraid of some preachers who come proclaiming another Jesus, a Lord other than the one that "husband" Paul preached. It is a seduction of the mind that Paul fears (contra Rom. 12:2), a leading astray of the people concerning the Gospel. People who come so preaching will be slick communicators, homiletical masters—Paul calls them "super-apostles." They will know how to work the crowds with their facile speech. Undoubtedly, they will be a great success in the pulpits of power. But in the knowledge of God and the Gospel they will fall far short of the mark. For that reason, they are so dangerous and must be resisted.

Throughout the New Testament we find the young church having to resist wrong theologies and dangerous spiritualities. "Beloved, do not believe every spirit, but test the spirits to see whether they are from God; for many false prophets have gone out into the world" (1 John 4:1). Again: "See to it that no one takes you captive through philosophy and empty deceit, according to human tradition, according to the elemental spirits of the universe, and not according to Christ" (Col. 2:8). In Mark's Gospel we find the same disdain for error in theology and spirituality: "And then if anyone says, 'Look, here is Christ!' or 'Look, there he is!' do not believe it. False christs and false prophets will arise and show signs and wonders, to lead astray, if possible, the elect" (13:21–22). Even if an angel from heaven should come preaching a false gospel, writes Paul, "let him be accursed." We need today a holy disbelief, a clarity of theological mind that leads us to reject everything named as spiritual that is not of the Gospel. The problem, perhaps, is that we all believe too much. We are too religious for our own good (Gal. 1:9). (See Ralph C. Wood, "In Defense of Disbelief," *First Things*, 96 [October 1998].)

Paul, in the face of this spiritual threat that reduces the Gospel to something other than the apostolic preaching, asserts his authority as the guardian of his people's life before God. He is their protector from the puerile spiritual myths that pass for truth, and the wrongheaded theological opinions that parade as knowledge. The task always is to contend for and to preach the faith once for all delivered to the saints (Jude 3).

Ordination to the ministry of the Word and sacraments of the Gospel and installation to be pastor of a congregation mean that one is charged to be a father (or, as the case may be, a mother) of the bride. In this sense the pastor is most rightly called "Father," or "Mother." According to the text for 2 Corinthians 11, the pastor has then two functional responsibilities: first, to preach, teach, and celebrate the Word of God rightly—to center the common life around Jesus who is Lord; and second, to protect the flock given into the pastor's charge from the seductions of the proprietors of what Paul called "another Jesus." That done, the pastor will, at the coming of the Lord Jesus Christ, present the flock as a bride, holy and sanctified, to her true husband. If the pastors do not do this, they are liable for the loss of the souls of their people.

Eternity is at stake. God will not be mocked. For a minister of the Gospel who has not been faithful to fall into the hands of a holy God is indeed a fearful and terrible thing. I pray to almighty God that you will be faithful in preaching the true Word of God, who is Jesus Christ our Lord, and that you will thereby protect your people from false teachers who would lead them astray.

To Jesus Christ, who loves us and has set us free from our sins with his blood, who has made of us a royal house to serve as the priests of his God and father—to him be the glory and dominion for ever (Rev. 1:5–6)!

Notes

Introduction

1. Jaroslav Pelikan notes that from 100 to 600, most theologians were bishops; from 600 to 1500, in the West, they were monks; and since 1500, they have been university professors! Jaroslav Pelikan, *The Emergence of the Catholic Tradition (100–600)* (Chicago: The University of Chicago Press, 1971), 5. I found this reference in R. A. Krupp, *Shepherding the Flock: The Pastoral Theology of John Chrysostom* (New York: Peter Lang, 1991), 3.
2. Note the subtitle to Brooks Holifield, *A History of Pastoral Care in America: From Salvation to Self-Realization* (Nashville: Abingdon Press, 1983).
3. Ellen T. Charry, *By the Renewing of Your Mind* (New York: Oxford University Press, 1987), 6.
4. C. S. Lewis, "Introduction." To Athanasius, *On the Incarnation*, trans. and ed. by a religious of C. S. M. V. (Crestwood, N.Y.: St. Vladimir's Seminary Press, 1982), 4.
5. L. O. Mills, "Pastoral Care (History, Traditions, and Definitions)," in Rodney J. Hunter, general editor, *Dictionary of Pastoral Care and Counseling* (Nashville: Abingdon Press, 1990), 836.
6. A number of pastoral theologians have made note of this point. See especially Alastair V. Campbell, *Rediscovering Pastoral Care* (London: Darton, Longman and Todd, 1981); Stephen Pattison, *A Critique of Pastoral Care* (London: SCM, 1988); Eugene H. Peterson, *Five Smooth Stones for Pastoral Work* (Atlanta: John Knox Press, 1980); Francis Bridger and David Atkinson, *Counselling in Context* (London: Harper Collins, 1994); and Thomas C. Oden, *Pastoral Theology* (San Francisco: Harper and Row, 1983), and *Care of Souls in the Classic Tradition* (Philadelphia: Fortress Press, 1984).
7. Bridger and Atkinson, *Counselling in Context*, op. cit., 5.
8. These examples are taken from William A. Clebsch and Charles R. Jaekle, *Pastoral Care in Historical Perspective: An Essay with Exhibits* (New York: Harper and Row, Publishers, 1967). For a more recent, and more extensive, collection see Philip L. Culbertson and Arthur Bradford Shippee, eds., *The Pastor: Readings from the Patristic Period* (Minneapolis: Fortress Press, 1990).
9. Thomas C. Oden, *Pastoral Theology: Essentials of Ministry* (San Francisco: Harper & Row, 1983), his four-volume *Classic Pastoral Care*, and *Pastoral Care in the Classic Tradition*; op. cit.; Carl A. Volz, *Pastoral Life and Practice in the Early Church* (Minneapolis: Augsburg Publishing House, 1990).
10. This trajectory is quite ignored by Clebsch and Jaekle, and is given only cursory treatment in John T. McNeill, *A History of the Cure of Souls* (New York: Harper and Row, Publishers, 1951), an otherwise useful survey. Culbertson and Shippee give some space to Chrysostom and Gregory the Great, but surprisingly omit the work of Gregory of Nazianzus on the priesthood, on which these Fathers build.

For brief but uncritical reviews, see Joseph T. Allen, *The Ministry of the Church* (Crestwood, N.Y.: St. Vladimir's Seminary Press, 1986), 69f., and Lewis J. Patsavos, "The Image of the Priest According to the Three Hierarchs," *Greek Orthodox Theological Review* XXI (spring, 1976).

11. In the Byzantine Church, St. Basil the Great of Caesarea, St. Gregory of Nazianzus, the Theologian, and St. John Chrysostom are the Three Holy Hierarchs and Universal Teachers who, along with St. Athanasius of Alexandria, are the four great *doctores ecclesiae* according to the Western church.

12. A case could be made for including Gilbert Burnet, *Discourse on the Pastoral Care*, ed., Robert D. Cornwall (Lewiston/Queenston/Lampeter: Edwin Mellen Press, 1997). However, while a new edition of this work is now available, it is not as well known nor has it been as influential as Baxter's *The Reformed Pastor*.

13. James I. Packer, *A Quest for Holiness: The Puritan Vision of the Christian Life* (Wheaton, Ill.: Crossway Books, 1990), 16.

Chapter 1

1. Brief but useful introductions to the life of Gregory of Nazianzus may be found in Georges Florovsky, *The Collected Works, Volume Seven: The Eastern Fathers of the Fourth Century* (Buchervertriebsanstalt, Postfach 461, FL-9490 Vaduz, Europa), 108f; Johannes Quasten, *Patrology* III (Westminster, Md.: The Newman Press, 1960), 236f.; Frederick W. Norris, "Introduction" to *Faith Gives Fullness to Reasoning: The Five Theological Orations of Gregory Nazianzen* (Leiden: E. J. Brill, 1991); Donald F. Winslow, *The Dynamics of Salvation: A Study in Gregory of Nazianzus* (Cambridge, Mass.: The Philadelphia Patristic Foundation, Ltd., 1979), chap. 1; and "Prolegomena," *A Select Library of Nicene and Post-Nicene Fathers of the Christian Church*, Second Series, eds. Philip Schaff and Henry Wace, vol. 7 (Edinburgh: T & T Clark, and Grand Rapids: Wm. B. Eerdmans, 1989), 187f.

2. Quasten, op. cit., 236.

3. Brooks Otis, "The Throne and the Mountain: An Essay on St. Gregory Nazianzus," *Classical Journal* 56 (1961).

4. Norris, op. cit., 1.

5. For a brief account, see Winslow, op. cit, 4–5.

6. Ibid., 6.

7. Florovsky, op. cit., 110.

8. Winslow, op. cit., 7.

9. Cited in Florovsky, op. cit., 110.

10. Florovsky, op. cit., 111.

11. Oration 10.1, cited by Winslow, op. cit, 9.

12. Florovsky, op. cit., 112.

13. Norris, op. cit., 8.

14. Florovsky, op. cit., 112.

15. Cited in Winslow, op. cit., 12.

16. See also *Or.* 2.35. For a recent translation of Gregory's *Theological Orations*, see Norris, op. cit.

17. For a general statement and extended argument, see T. F. Torrance, *The Trinitarian Faith* (Edinburgh: T & T Clark, 1993), 17 and following.

18. Gregory Naz., *Or.* 27.3. While the statement holds up in its own right, we note however, that Gregory's family was wealthy. Winslow refers to Gregory's "almost aristocratic insistence," op. cit., 27.

19. A helpful introduction is given by Winslow, op. cit., chap. 2.
20. Torrance, op. cit, 321.
21. John D. Zizioulas, *Being as Communion: Studies in Personhood and the Church* (London: Darton, Longman and Todd, 1985), 27.
22. Quasten, op. cit., 252.
23. Gregory Naz., *Epistle*, 101. See also *Or.* 37.2.
24. See also *Or* 38.9–11.
25. Allen, op. cit., 70f., identifies four aspects for discussion: the shepherd as doctor in pastoral care, the maturity and propriety of the shepherd, the shepherd and the teaching of doctrine, and the need for training and experience.
26. Ibid., 70.
27. I am indebted to Nan Chalfont-Walker, a student at Pittsburgh Theological Seminary, for the first draft of this outline.

Chapter 2

1. Philip Schaff, "The Life and Work of St. John Chrysostom," Prolegomena to P. Schaff, ed., *Nicene and Post-Nicene Fathers of the Christian Church*, vol. IX (New York: The Christian Literature Company, 1889), 22.
2. Yet it may have been likely insofar as Flavian, the Bishop of Antioch who ordained him a priest, had been appointed, albeit against his wishes, during the time when Gregory was bishop of Constantinople.
3. Schaff, op. cit., 16; see also J. N. D. Kelly, *Golden Mouth: The Story of John Chrysostom—Ascetic, Preacher, Bishop* (Ithaca, N.Y.: Cornell University Press, 1995), 106.
4. Kelly, op. cit., 4.
5. Schaff, op. cit., 5; see also Kelly, op. cit., 7.
6. AD 349 is the date that best fits the known facts, although this cannot be fixed exactly. See Kelly, op. cit., 4.
7. Ibid., 9.
8. Ibid., 15. See also St. John Chrysostom, *Six Books on the Priesthood*, trans. Graham Neville (Crestwood, N.Y.: St. Vladimir's Seminary Press, 1984), 83–84, and "Treatise on the Priesthood," III.13–III.14 in *Nicene and Post-Nicene Fathers*, IX. Hereafter cited respectively in the text by a page number reference to Neville's translation and a paragraph reference to the NPNF edition.
9. Cited by Schaff, op. cit., 6.
10. Cited by Kelly, op. cit., 17.
11. Robert Payne, T*he Fathers of the Eastern Church* (New York: Dorset Press, 1989), 197.
12. Kelly, op. cit., 106.
13. Cited by William Bright, *Lessons from the Lives of Three Great Fathers* (London: Longmans, Green & Co., 1891), 75.
14. Cited by Schaff, op. cit., 14.
15. Cited by Bright, op. cit., 92.
16. See J. Quasten, *Patrology*, Vol. 3 (Westminster, Maryland: The Newman Press, 1960), 429, and Schaff, op. cit., 17.
17. For a useful, though somewhat technical, summary, see George Hendry, "Christology" in Alan Richardson, ed., *A Doctionary of Christian Theology* (Philadelphia: The Westminster Press, 1969).
18. For much of what follows, see Christopher A. Hall, *Reading Scripture with the Church Fathers* (Downers Grove, Ill.: InterVarsity Press, 1988), chaps. 6 and 7.
19. Ibid., 132.

20. Ibid., 133.
21. Thus Schaff, op. cit., 18. Hall calls the method "hermeneutical dynamite," op. cit., 156.
22. Andrew Louth, *Discerning the Mystery: An Essay on the Nature of Theology* (Oxford: Clarendon Press, 1983), 96.
23. Ibid., 107.
24. Ibid., 111.
25. Louth calls it "an alliance between the Reformation and the Enlightenment: not something that inspires confidence," ibid., 101.
26. See by Hall, who cites Karlfried Froelich, op. cit., 157.
27. Hall, citing Joseph Trigg, op. cit., 158.
28. Ibid., 166.
29. Quasten, op. cit., 433.
30. *Nicene and Post-Nicene Fathers of the Christian Church*, ed. Schaff, vol. X; John Chrysostom, *The Homilies of St. John Chrysostom on the Gospel of St. Matthew*, trans. George Prevost (New York: The Christian Literature Company, 1888), 20.
31. Hall. op. cit., 96.
32. Cited from Homily 7 on Philippians in Quasten, op. cit., 475.
33. Schaff, op. cit., 20.
34. Quasten, op. cit., 480, although arguably his interpretation at this point pushes in the direction of a Roman perspective. See Schaff, op. cit., 21.
35. From Chrysostom's homily on Matthew, LXXXII, cited by A Monk of the Eastern Church, *Orthodox Spirituality: An Outline of the Orthodox Ascetical and Mystical Tradition*, 2d ed. (Crestwood, N.Y.: St. Vladimir's Seminary Press, 1996), 83.
36. Quasten, op. cit., 480–81.
37. "The chief object of the composition was to place the greatness and responsibility of the priesthood in the right light." Quasten, op. cit., 462.
38. See Richard Valantasis, "Body, Hierarchy, and Leadership in Chrysostom's *On the Priesthood*," *Greek Orthodox Theological Review*, 30, no. 4 (1985), 455–71, for what follows.
39. "Our struggle is not against enemies of blood and flesh, but against the rulers, against the authorities, against the cosmic powers of this present darkness, against the spiritual forces of evil in the heavenly places."

Chapter 3

1. Thomas C. Oden, *Care of Souls in the Classic Tradition* (Philadelphia: Fortress Press, 1984), 115. This is also the place to pay tribute to Oden's pioneering work on classical pastoral care. For many this book was our introduction to the classical past in pastoral theology.
2. Oden, *Pastoral Care in the Classic Tradition*, 43.
3. Oddly, G. R. Evans gives his birth date as ca. 550, in contradiction to every other source investigated, *The Thought of Gregory the Great* (London: Cambridge University Press, 1986), 4.
4. *Bede's Ecclesiastical History of the English People*, II.1, eds., Bertram Colgrave and R. A. B. Mynors (Oxford: The Clarendon Press, 1969), 123.
5. See Carole Straw, *Gregory the Great: Perfection in Imperfection* (Berkeley: University of California Press, 1988), 2.
6. G. Roger Hudleston, "Pope St. Gregory ('the Great')," at www.newadvent.org (1909).
7. It is not clear whether or not these youths were slaves. The Venerable Bede says

that they were boys put up for sale, in *Bede's Ecclesiastical History*, II.1, 133.

8. *Bede's Ecclesiastical History*, II.1, 123.
9. Catherine Goddard Clark, "The Life of Saint Gregory the Great," www.catholicism.org/pages/greg.htm.
10. Evans, op. cit., 24.
11. *Bede's Ecclesiastical History*, II.1, 133.
12. "Gregory is a theologian without deep intellectual anxieties." Evans, op. cit., 55.
13. Straw, op. cit., 9.
14. Evans, op. cit., 46.
15. Straw, op. cit., 65.
16. For the following see Evans, op. cit., 19f.
17. This is a major theme of Straw, op. cit., and references may be found throughout her book.
18. Henceforth citations of Gregory's *Pastoral Care* will be given in this way. The first reference is to the Book and Chapter, the second to the page in *Gregory the Great: Regula Pastoralis*, trans. and annotated by Henry Davis, S.J. (New York: Newman Press, 1978), vol, 11, *Ancient Christian Writers: The Works of the Fathers in Translation*, eds. Johannes Quasten and Joseph C. Plumpe.
19. Cited by Evans, op. cit., 25.
20. Cited by Straw, op. cit., 108.
21. Ibid., 109.
22. Ibid., 178.
23. Cited by Henry Davis, S. J., "Introduction," *St. Gregory the Great: Pastoral Care*, 10.
24. Davis, "Introduction," 11.
25. H. R. Bramley, *St. Gregory on the Pastoral Charge: the Benedictine Text, with an English Translation* (Oxford, 1874), ix.
26. F. Homes Dudden, *Gregory the Great: His Place in History and Thought*, vol. 1 (New York: Longmans, Green, and Co., 1905), 230.
27. Oden, *Care of Souls in the Classic Tradition*, 65.
28. See Andrew Purves, *The Search for Compassion* (Louisville: Westminster John Knox Press, 1989).
29. Oden, *Care of Souls in the Classic Tradition*, 72.
30. It would be too tedious to work our way through the thirty-six antinomies. Oden has already done that for us in *Care of Souls in the Classic Tradition*, chaps. 3 and 4.
31. Ibid., 78.

Chapter 4

1. Translated from *Von der waren Seelsorge* by W. P. Stephens, *The Holy Spirit in the Theology of Martin Bucer* (Cambridge: Cambridge University Press, 1970), 162.
2. I first read *Von der waren Seelsorge* in an unpublished English translation by Peter J. Beale when I was asked by Professor David F. Wright of the University of Edinburgh to write an introduction to Bucer's pastoral theology for a projected publication of Beale's translation. At the time of writing that translation has not yet been published. Subsequently I have consulted the German edition of *Von der waren Seelsorge*, and references are to Robert Stupperich, ed., *Martin Bucers Deutsche Schriften, Band 7: Schriften der Jahre 1538–1539* (Gutersloh and Paris: 1964), 90–241. References to *Von der waren Seelsorge* will give the page number and the line on which the citation begins. Some references are to marginal headings in the German text; these are similarly documented, but not otherwise identified.
3. Unlike the other chapters, this chapter has almost no direct quotations from the prin-

cipal text, there being no published English translation. Occasionally where I do cite
the text to make a specific point, the English is followed by the German original.

4. J. T. McNeill, *A History of the Cure of Souls* (New York: Harper & Brothers, 1951),
177. Wilhelm Pauck uses almost identical language: "The most outstanding book
of this kind was a work of Martin Bucer. . . ." *The Heritage of the Reformation*, (London: Oxford University Press, 1961), 107.

5. McNeill, op. cit., 180.

6. W. P. Stephens, op. cit., 193.

7. David F. Wright, "Martin Bucer 1491–1551: Ecumenical Theologian," in Wright,
trans. and ed., *Common Places of Martin Bucer* (Abingdon, England: Sutton Courte-
nay Press, 1972), 21.

8. Thomas F. Torrance, *Kingdom and Church* (Edinburgh: Oliver and Boyd, 1956),
73.

9. Ibid., 75.

10. Amy Nelson Burnett, *The Yoke of Christ: Martin Bucer and Christian Discipline*
(Kirksville, Mo.: Sixteenth Century Journal Publishers, vol. XXVI, 1994), 87.

11. William A. Clebsch and Charles R. Jaekle, *Pastoral Care in Historical Perspective:
An Essay with Exhibits* (New York: Harper & Row, 1967). These writers do make
a useful introductory point, however: "Pastoral care today is undergoing swift and
sweeping transition. This transition begs a necessity to appropriate and appreciate the lore of a long and fruitful experience of Christian pastors in helping troubled people. To their methods and aims we are no more bound than we are able
actually to re-enter their particular circumstances. Yet history knows no absolute
discontinuities, and much that we might take to be new methods of soul care we
may learn to be mere variations upon time-honored approaches to the task," 2–3.

12. Thomas F. Torrance, "The Eschatology of the Reformation," in *Eschatology: Scottish Journal of Theology Occasional Papers No. 2* (Edinburgh: Oliver and Boyd Ltd.,
1953), 53.

13. David C. Steinmetz, *Reformers in the Wings* (Philadelphia: Fortress Press, 1971), 121.

14. Hastings Eells, *Martin Bucer* (New Haven: Yale University Press, 1931), 415–16.
After her death during the plague of 1541 Bucer married Wibrandis, the widow
of Wolfgang Capito, who outlived him by more than a decade.

15. Thus Wright, *Common Places of Martin Bucer*, 11.

16. See, for example, the discussion by Stephens, op. cit., 56, where he notes Bucer's
theological method with regard to faith and works in the context of justification.

17. Martin Bucer, "A Brief Summary of Christian Doctrine," in Wright, op. cit.. 78.

18. Ibid., 79.

19. Stephens, op. cit., 38.

20. Ibid., 49.

21. Martin Bucer, "Justification," in Wright, op. cit., 166.

22. Ibid., 171.

23. Bucer, in Ibid., 172.

24. Cited by Stephens, op. cit., 65.

25. Bucer, in Wright, op. cit., 177.

26. Torrance, op. cit., 82.

27. Stephens, op. cit., 91.

28. Ibid., 66.

29. Wright, op. cit., 34.

30. For the genesis of this metaphor, see Wright, ibid., 32.

31. Martin Bucer, *A Brief Summary of Christian Doctrine*, in Wright, op. cit., 87.

32. Bucer mistranslates the end of the verse to read, "to guard/look after the fat and the strong and feed them rightly." McNeill, *A History of the Cure of Souls*, makes note of this mistranslation, 178. For Bucer's use see *Von der waren Seelsorge*, (93,1 and 141,35).

33. Stephens, op. cit., 147.

34. See, for example, Hiltner's major texts, *Preface to Pastoral Theology* (Nashville: Abingdon Press, 1958) and *The Christian Shepherd* (New York: Abingdon Press, 1959). For a standard critique, see Thomas C. Oden, *Contemporary Theology and Psychotherapy* (Philadelphia: The Westminster Press, 1967), 90–91.

35. Thomas C. Oden, *Pastoral Theology: Essentials of Ministry* (San Francisco: Harper and Row, 1983); William B. Oglesby, Jr., *Biblical Themes for Pastoral Care* (Nashville: Abingdon Press, 1980); Eugene H. Peterson, *Five Smooth Stones for Pastoral Work* (Atlanta: John Knox Press, 1980); Eduard Thurneysen, *A Theology of Pastoral Care*, basic translation by Jack A. Worthington and Thomas Wieser, assisted by a panel of advisers (Richmond: John Knox Press, 1962); and Donald Capps, *Biblical Approaches to Pastoral Counseling* (Philadelpia: The Westminster Press, 1981) among others merit mention. See also Andrew Purves, *The Search for Compassion: Spirituality and Ministry* (Louisville: Westminster John Knox Press, 1989). A list of books by Jay Adams could also be given here, though he tends to represent a much more conservative position, while the authors cited represent mainline Protestant denominations.

36. In Rodney J. Hunter, general editor, *Dictionary of Pastoral Care and Counseling* (Nashville: Abingdon Press, 1990), the article on christology and pastoral care struggles to list more than a very few books on christology in the quite extensive bibliography.

37. Howard Clinebell, *Basic Types of Pastoral Care and Counseling* (Nashville: Abingdon Press, 1984), 67, 103.

38. W. J. Lowe, "Christology and Pastoral Care," in Hunter, ed., *Dictionary of Pastoral Care and Counseling*, 157.

39. Clebsch and Jaekle, *Pastoral Care in Historical Perspective*, 4, 11f., and 32f.

40. "In the Rhineland Martin Bucer, and after him John Calvin, developed systems of ecclesiastical discipline that worked out in detail the ways in which reconciliation of the believer with God involved reconciliation with his fellow believers." Ibid., 27.

41. Bucer in Wright, op. cit., 120.

42. See Stephens, op. cit., 24–25.

43. Ibid., 48–49.

44. E. Brooks Holifield, *A History of Pastoral Care in America: From Salvation to Self-Realization* (Nashville: Abingdon Press, 1983).

45. See, for example, John Patton, *Pastoral Care in Context: An Introduction to Pastoral Care*, (Louisville: Westminster John Knox Press, 1993), 16. The index contains no listing under "sin."

46. See, however, the effort of Don S. Browning to introduce moral discourse into pastoral theology, in "Pastoral Theology in a Pluralistic Age," in *Practical Theology*, Don S. Browning, ed. (New York: Harper and Row, 1983).

47. This is a well-known criticism: see, for example, A. V. Campbell, "Is Practical Theology Possible?" *Scottish Journal of Theology*, vol. 25 (May 1972).

Chapter 5

1. Cited in Hugh Martin, *Puritanism and Richard Baxter* (London: SCM Press, 1954), 17. This brief account of the movement is taken in part from Martin's account.

2. Ibid., 76.
3. James I. Packer, *A Quest for Godliness: The Puritan Vision of the Christian Life* (Wheaton, Ill.: Crossway Books, 1990), 304.
4. Richard Baxter, *The Autobiography of Richard Baxter*, ed., N. H. Keeble (Totowa, N.J.: Rowman and Littlefield, 1974) 12.
5. Geoffrey F. Nuttall, *Richard Baxter* (London: Thomas Nelson and Sons, 1965) 43.
6. Baxter, op. cit., 11.
7. Ibid., 76.
8. Ibid., 5.
9. Ibid., 9.
10. Richard Baxter, *The Reformed Pastor*, ed. William Brown (Edinburgh: The Banner of Truth Trust, 1979), 56. The book was published first in 1656.
11. Nuttall, op. cit., 5.
12. Ibid., 47.
13. Packer, op. cit., 28
14. Ibid., 65.
15. Ibid., 157.
16. Ibid., 49.
17. Baxter, *The Reformed Pastor*, 53.
18. James I. Packer, "Introduction," to Richard Baxter, *The Reformed Pastor*, 12.
19. John von Rohr, *The Covenant of Grace in Puritan Thought* (Atlanta: Scholars Press, 1986), 97.
20. Ibid., 98–100.
21. From Richard Baxter, *Justifying Righteousness*, cited by von Rohr, op. cit., 99.
22. From Richard Baxter, *Of Justification*, cited by von Rohr, op. cit., 99.
23. Richard Baxter, *Justifying Righteousness*, cited by von Rohr, op. cit., 100.
24. James I. Packer, op. cit., 159.
25. John Macleod, *Scottish Theology*, cited in James I. Packer, "Introduction," to Richard Baxter, *The Reformed Pastor*, op. cit., 10.
26. Packer, *A Quest for Godliness*, 160.
27. Baxter, *The Reformed Pastor*, 133.
28. See reference in Baxter, *Autobiography*, 97.
29. Richard Baxter, *The Reformed Pastor*, 37.
30. Noted by Charles F. Kemp, *A Pastoral Triumph: The Story of Richard Baxter and His Ministry at Kidderminster* (New York: The Macmillan Company, 1948), 42.
31. Martin, *op. cit.* 152.
32. Baxter, *Autobiography*, 97.
33. Baxter, *The Reformed Pastor*, 132.
34. Ibid., 133.
35. Ibid., 62.
36. Ibid., 53.
37. Ibid., 72.
38. Ibid., 61.
39. Ibid., 62.
40. Ibid., 63.
41. Ibid., 81.
42. Ibid., 75.
43. Ibid., 143.
44. Ibid., 144, 145.
45. Ibid., 143.

46. Ibid., 146.
47. Ibid., 148–49.
48. Ibid., 150.
49. Ibid., 74.
50. Ibid., 73.
51. Ibid., 176.
52. Ibid., 41.
53. Ibid., 125.
54. Ibid., 111.
55. Ibid., 94.
56. Ibid., 95.
57. Ibid., 149.
58. Ibid., 95.
59. James I. Packer, "Introduction" to Baxter, *The Reformed Pastor*, 10.
60. Baxter, *The Reformed Pastor*, 174.
61. John von Rohr, op. cit., 54.
62. Ibid., 54.
63. Baxter, *The Reformed Pastor*, 91.
64. Ibid., 88.
65. Ibid., 156.
66. Ibid., 130.
67. Ibid., 132.
68. Cited by Nuttall, op. cit., 57–58. See also Baxter, *The Reformed Pastor*, 183, and Baxter, *Autobiography*, 77.
69. Baxter, *The Reformed Pastor*, 184.
70. Ibid., 180.
71. Ibid., 43.
72. Cited by Nuttall, op. cit., 59.
73. Baxter, *The Reformed Pastor*, 43.
74. Baxter, *Autobiography*, 79.
75. Ibid.

Index